ATLAS OF ANCIENT HISTORY

ATLAS OF ANCIENT HISTORY

Michael Grant
Cartography by ARTHUR BANKS

Revised Edition

DORSET PRESS

Formerly published as *Ancient History Atlas*

This edition published by Dorset Press, a division of
Marboro Books Corp., by arrangement with the Macmillan
Publishing Company.

1985 Dorset Press

ISBN 0-88029-009-9
(Previously ISBN 0-02-545130-8)

Printed and bound in the United States of America

Preface

This is, in the first place, an atlas of the classical world – the ancient Greek and Roman world, which needs to be understood if we are to understand the world of today. To say that such an atlas could ever be a substitute for a historical survey would be an exaggeration. Nevertheless, geography is such a vital, indeed predominant, factor in ancient history – and such a difficult factor because of all the changes of names[1] – that the whole course of events often seems to mean practically nothing without maps, and without a lot of them, carefully devised.

Older classical atlases, apart from a varying degree of emphasis on physical aspects, tended to concentrate on political themes, and it is true enough that these stand in great need of maps. But the present volume attempts to cast the net wider, and to introduce economic, cultural, religious and other topics as well. There are also a number of town plans.

Modern research in archaeology and other fields has shown that the classical world cannot be grasped without some appreciation of what went before it. I have consequently started this book with a number of maps illustrating the Mediterranean world during the second millennium BC, and particularly during the period from 1700 BC onwards, when the international scene had already assumed a well-defined and complex appearance; and the story is carried onwards to offer brief illustrations of the Old Testament. At the other end of the story, the traditional terminal date of the ancient world, the year AD 476 when the last western emperor ceased to reign, is again not a very meaningful landmark, so I have carried on the tale until the reign of Justinian in the following century.

It will be clear enough what a very great deal is owed to the talent of Mr Arthur Banks for transcribing the written and spoken word into cartographic form. I am also most grateful to Mr Julian Shuckburgh for all the assistance he has rendered on behalf of the publishers, and I want to thank Miss Jane Dorner for assistance with the index and Mr C. R. B. Elliott for help with the latest revised edition. Finally, I have to acknowledge a substantial debt to existing classical atlases, German and English. And I must single out, for a special word of gratitude, the *Atlas of the Classical World* edited by A. A. M. van der Heyden and H. H. Scullard for Messrs Nelson, and *Westermanns Grosser Atlas zur Weltgeshchichte* (Westermann, Braunschweig). N. G. L. Hammond's *Atlas of the Greek and Roman World in Antiquity* (Noyes Press, Park Ridge) is now fundamental.

1971, 1974, 1985   MICHAEL GRANT

[1] Modern names are given after the ancient in the Index.

List of Maps

0
100
Miles

Kuban

Maiko[p]

BLACK SEA

Burials c. 2300

TROY
• Dorak

Sangarios
Halys

• Alacahüyük
HATTUSAS •

HITTITES
• Alisarhüyük

Kanesh •

• Keban
Malatya •

BEYCESULTAN
Maeander
Miletus •
• Aphrodisias

Can Hasan •
• Karatepe
ADANA •
Mersin •
Tarsus

• Edessa
CARCHEMISH
AMIK
• Haran
• Alalakh
Euphrate[s]
• ALEPPO

CYPRUS
Ugarit •
Orontes
• Hamath
• Idalium
• QATNA
Kadesh •
• Homs

BYBLOS •

• Damascus

• Dan
HAZOR •
• Megiddo

Syrian

Desert

• Gezer
Gaza •
• Hebron

Nile

HYKSOS
EGYPT
• MEMPHIS

1

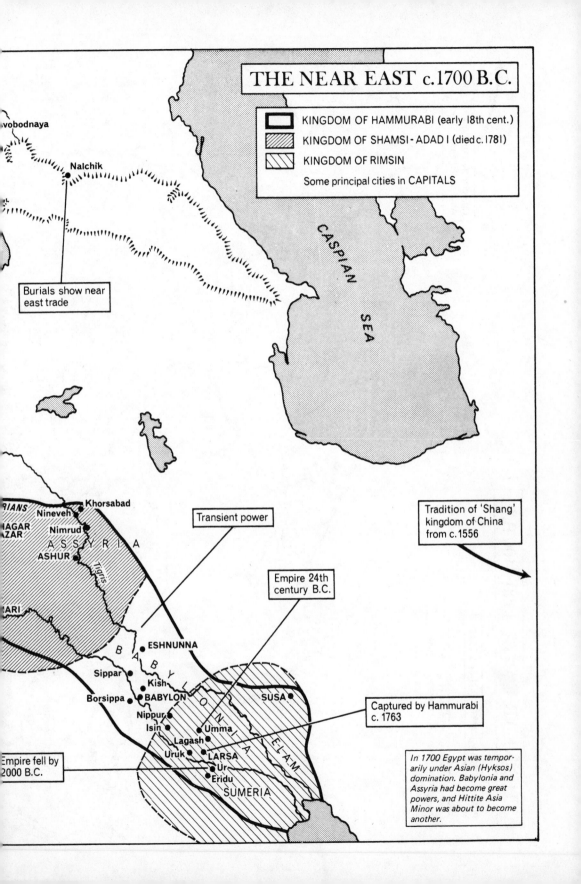

THE NEAR EAST c.1700 B.C.

KINGDOM OF HAMMURABI (early 18th cent.)

KINGDOM OF SHAMSI-ADAD I (died c.1781)

KINGDOM OF RIMSIN

Some principal cities in CAPITALS

vobodnaya

Nalchik

CASPIAN SEA

Burials show near east trade

Khorsabad
Nineveh
Nimrud
ASSYRIA
ASHUR

RIANS
HAGAR
AZAR
ARI

Tigris

Transient power

Empire 24th century B.C.

Tradition of 'Shang' kingdom of China from c.1556

ESHNUNNA

BABYLONIA

Sippar
Kish
Borsippa
BABYLON
Nippur
Isin
Umma
Lagash
Uruk
LARSA
Ur
Eridu
SUMERIA

SUSA

ELAM

Captured by Hammurabi c.1763

Empire fell by 2000 B.C.

In 1700 Egypt was temporarily under Asian (Hyksos) domination. Babylonia and Assyria had become great powers, and Hittite Asia Minor was about to become another.

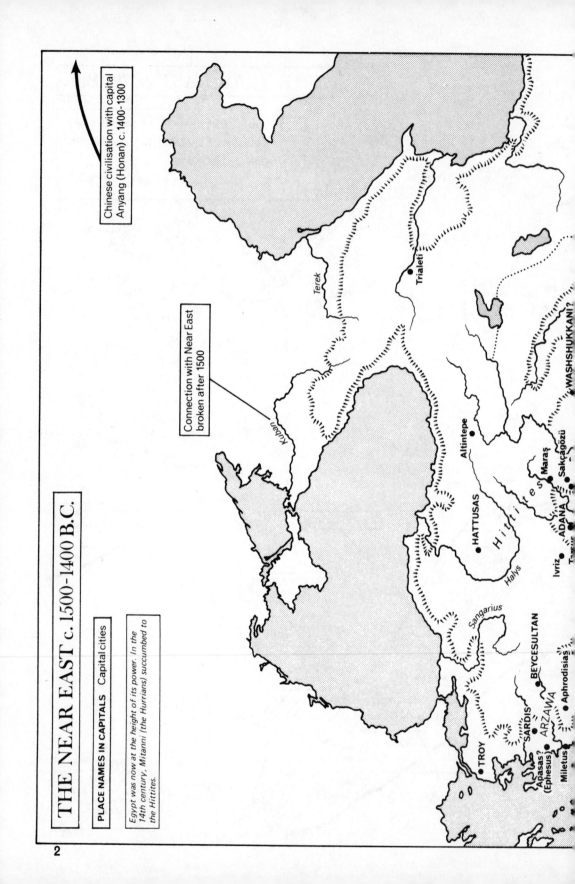

THE NEAR EAST c. 1500-1400 B.C.

PLACE NAMES IN CAPITALS Capital cities

Egypt was now at the height of its power. In the 14th century, Mitanni (the Hurrians) succumbed to the Hittites.

Chinese civilisation with capital Anyang (Honan) c. 1400-1300

Connection with Near East broken after 1500

Terek

Trialeti

Kuban

Altintepe

WASHSHUKKANI?

Maraş

Sakçagözü

H i t t i t e s

ADANA

HATTUSAS

Ivriz

Tarsus

Halys

Sangarius

BEYCESULTAN

SARDIS

ARZAWA

Aphrodisias

TROY

Apasas? (Ephesus)

Miletus

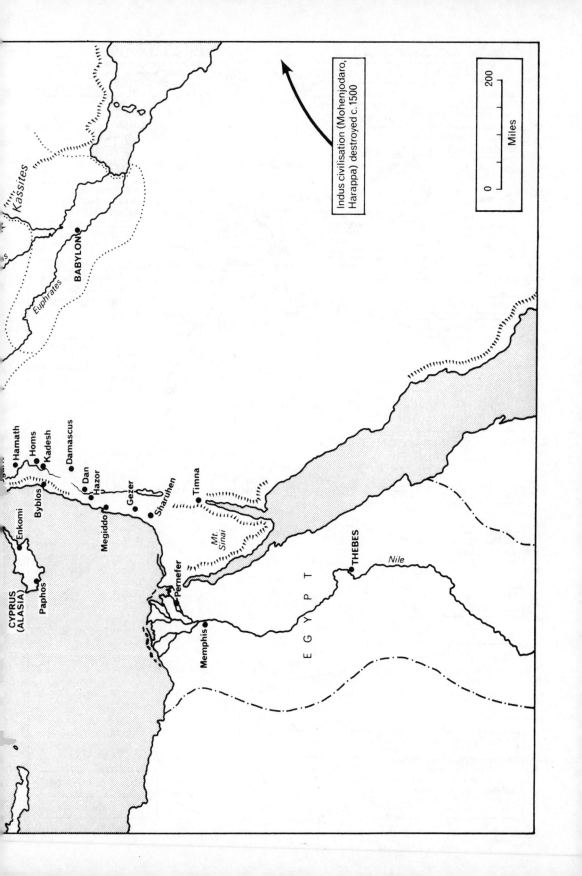

Indus civilisation (Mohenjodaro, Harappa) destroyed c.1500

0   200
Miles

Kassites

BABYLON

Euphrates

Hamath
Homs
Kadesh
Damascus

Dan
Hazor
Gezer
Sharuhen
Timna

Enkomi
Byblos
Megiddo

CYPRUS
(ALASIA)

Paphos

Mt.
Sinai

Pernefer

E G Y P T

THEBES
Nile

Memphis

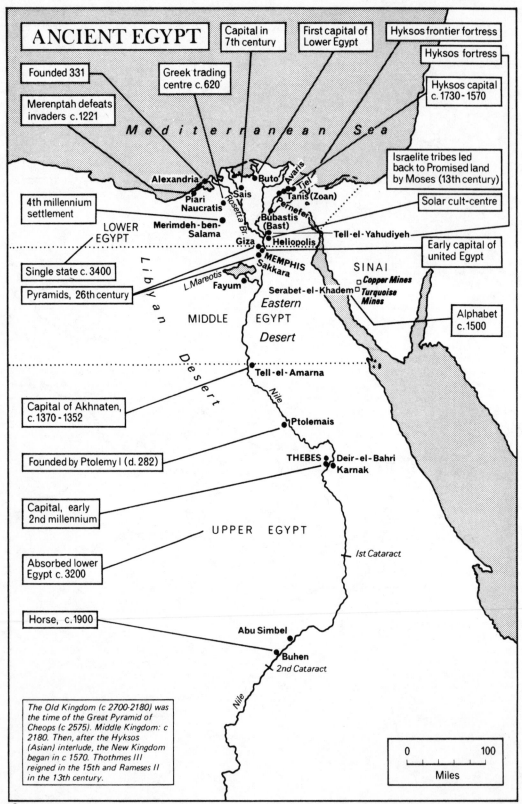

ANCIENT EGYPT

Founded 331

Merenptah defeats invaders c.1221

Capital in 7th century

Greek trading centre c.620

First capital of Lower Egypt

Hyksos frontier fortress

Hyksos fortress

Hyksos capital c.1730-1570

M e d i t e r r a n e a n   S e a

Israelite tribes led back to Promised land by Moses (13th century)

4th millennium settlement

Solar cult-centre

Alexandria

Buto

Avaris

Tjel

Sais

Tanis (Zoan)

Piari Naucratis

Rosetta Br.

Pernefer

Bubastis (Bast)

Tell-el-Yahudiyeh

LOWER EGYPT

Merimdeh-ben-Salama

Giza

Heliopolis

Early capital of united Egypt

Single state c.3400

MEMPHIS

Sakkara

S I N A I

□ Copper Mines

Pyramids, 26th century

L.Mareotis

Fayum

Serabet-el-Khadem

□ *Turquoise Mines*

L i b y a n

MIDDLE

Eastern EGYPT Desert

Alphabet c.1500

D e s e r t

Tell-el-Amarna

Nile

Capital of Akhnaten, c.1370-1352

Ptolemais

Founded by Ptolemy I (d.282)

THEBES

Deir-el-Bahri

Karnak

Capital, early 2nd millennium

U P P E R   E G Y P T

Ist Cataract

Absorbed lower Egypt c.3200

Horse, c.1900

Abu Simbel

Buhen

2nd Cataract

Nile

The Old Kingdom (c 2700-2180) was the time of the Great Pyramid of Cheops (c 2575). Middle Kingdom: c 2180. Then, after the Hyksos (Asian) interlude, the New Kingdom began in c 1570. Thothmes III reigned in the 15th and Rameses II in the 13th century.

0   100

Miles

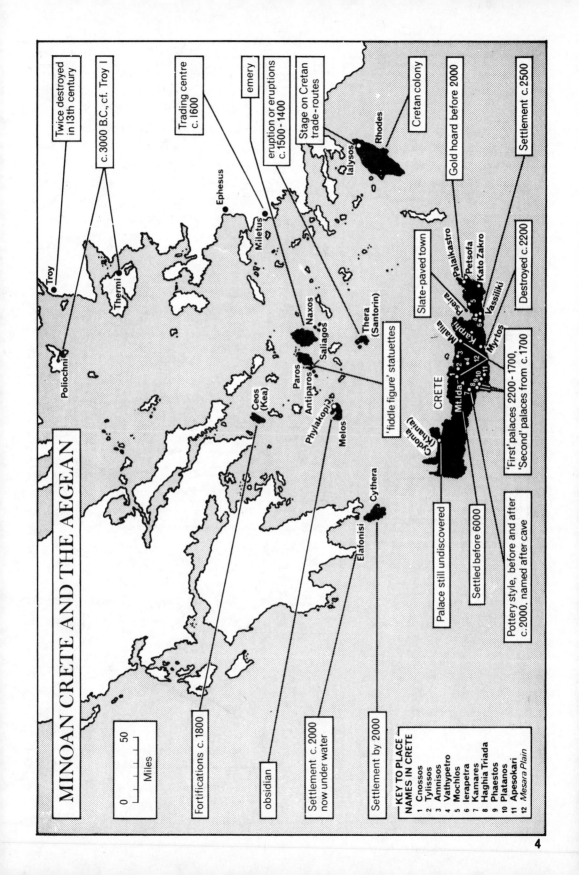

MINOAN CRETE AND THE AEGEAN

Twice destroyed in 13th century

c. 3000 B.C., cf. Troy I

Trading centre c. 1600

emery

eruption or eruptions c. 1500 - 1400

Stage on Cretan trade-routes

Cretan colony

Gold hoard before 2000

Settlement c. 2500

Destroyed c. 2200

Slate-paved town

'First' palaces 2200 - 1700, 'Second' palaces from c. 1700

Pottery style, before and after c. 2000, named after cave

Settled before 6000

Palace still undiscovered

Settlement by 2000

Settlement c. 2000 now under water

obsidian

Fortifications c. 1800

Troy

Poliochni

Thermi

Ephesus

Miletus

Rhodes

Ialysos

Naxos

Saliagos

Thera (Santorin)

Paros

Antiparos

Ceos (Kea)

Phylakopi

Melos

Elafonisi

Cythera

CRETE

Mt. Ida

Kydonia (Khania)

Mallia

Karphi

Pseira

Palaikastro

Petsofa

Kato Zakro

Vassiliki

Myrtos

0   50

Miles

KEY TO PLACE NAMES IN CRETE
1   Cnossos
2   Tylissos
3   Amnisos
4   Vathypetro
5   Mochlos
6   Ierapetra
7   Kamares
8   Haghia Triada
9   Phaestos
10 Platanos
11 Apesokari
12 *Mesara Plain*

4

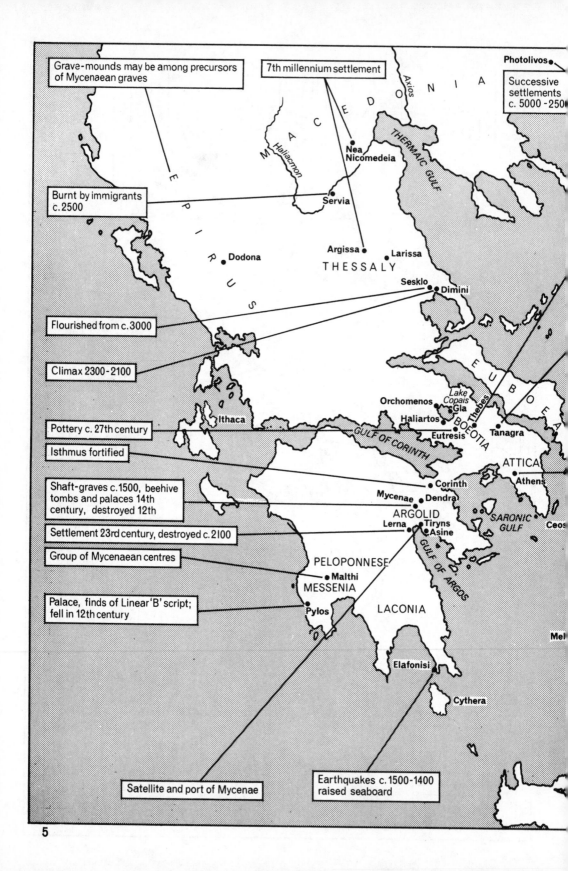

Grave-mounds may be among precursors of Mycenaean graves

7th millennium settlement

Photolivos

Successive settlements c. 5000 - 2500

M A C E D O N I A

Axios

Haliacmon

E P I R U S

Nea Nicomedeia

THERMAIC GULF

Burnt by immigrants c.2500

Servia

Dodona

Argissa

Larissa

THESSALY

Sesklo

Dimini

Flourished from c.3000

Climax 2300 - 2100

E U B O E A

Ithaca

Orchomenos

Lake Copais

Gla

Thebes

Haliartos

BOEOTIA

Eutresis

Tanagra

Pottery c. 27th century

GULF OF CORINTH

ATTICA

Isthmus fortified

Corinth

Athens

Shaft-graves c.1500, beehive tombs and palaces 14th century, destroyed 12th

Mycenae

Dendra

ARGOLID

Tiryns

SARONIC GULF

Ceos

Settlement 23rd century, destroyed c. 2100

Lerna

Asine

Group of Mycenaean centres

PELOPONNESE

GULF OF ARGOS

Malthi

MESSENIA

Palace, finds of Linear 'B' script; fell in 12th century

Pylos

LACONIA

Mel

Elafonisi

Cythera

Satellite and port of Mycenae

Earthquakes c. 1500-1400 raised seaboard

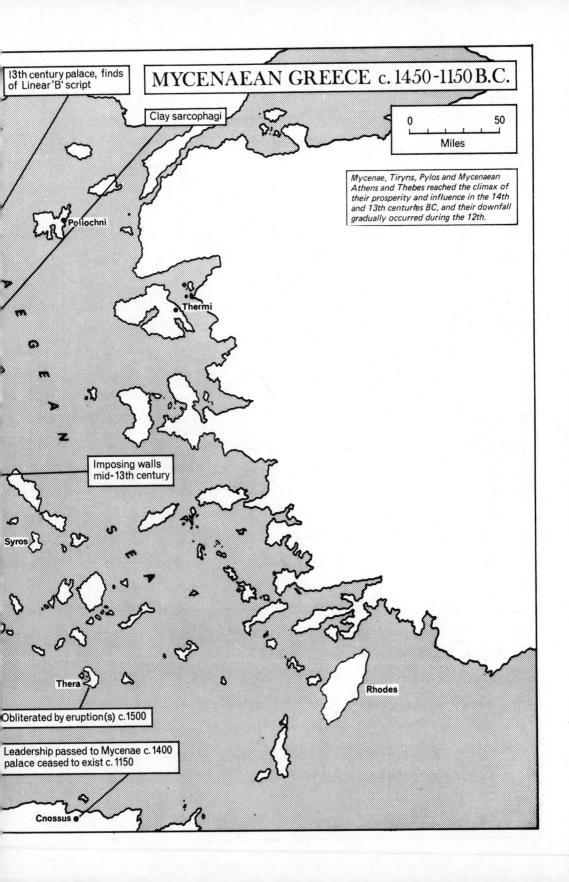

MYCENAEAN GREECE c. 1450-1150 B.C.

13th century palace, finds of Linear 'B' script

Clay sarcophagi

0   50

Miles

Mycenae, Tiryns, Pylos and Mycenaean Athens and Thebes reached the climax of their prosperity and influence in the 14th and 13th centuries BC, and their downfall gradually occurred during the 12th.

Poliochni

AEGEAN

Thermi

Imposing walls mid-13th century

SEA

Syros

Thera

Rhodes

Obliterated by eruption(s) c.1500

Leadership passed to Mycenae c.1400 palace ceased to exist c.1150

Cnossus

MYCENAEAN EXPANSION

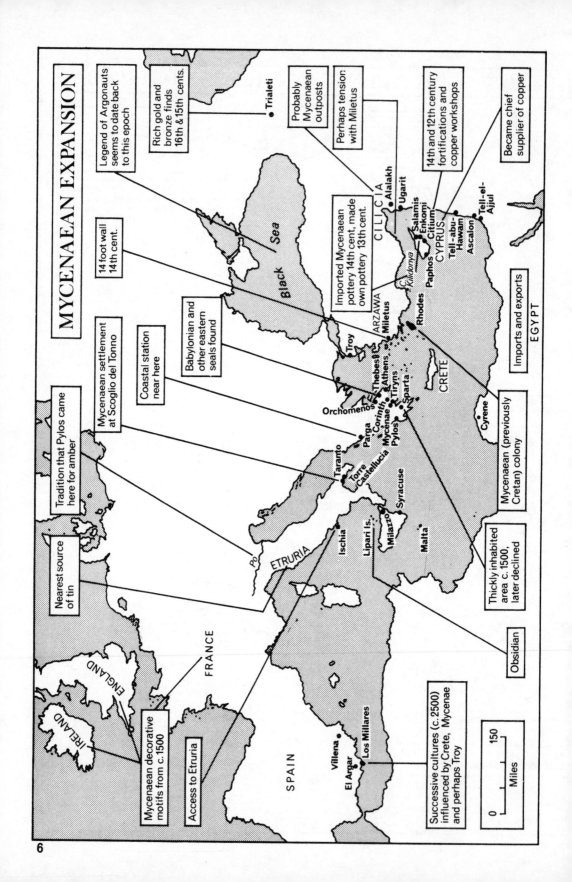

Rich gold and bronze finds 16th & 15th cents.

Legend of Argonauts seems to date back to this epoch

Trialeti

Probably Mycenaean outposts

Perhaps tension: with Miletus

14th and 12th century fortifications and copper workshops

Became chief supplier of copper

14 foot wall 14th cent.

Imported Mycenaean pottery 14th cent, made own pottery 13th cent.

CILICIA

Alalakh

Ugarit

Salamis

Enkomi

Citium?

CYPRUS

Paphos

Tell-abu-Hawam

Ascalon

Tell-el-Ajjul

Babylonian and other eastern seals found

Black Sea

ARZAWA

Kilidonya

Miletus

Troy

Rhodes

Coastal station near here

Mycenaean settlement at Scoglio del Tonno

Thebes

Athens

Orchomenos

Corinth

Mycenae

Tiryns

Sparta

Pylos

Parga

Taranto

Torre Castelluccia

CRETE

Cyrene

EGYPT

Imports and exports

Tradition that Pylos came here for amber

Mycenaean (previously Cretan) colony

Nearest source of tin

Syracuse

Ischia

Lipari Is.

Milazzo

Malta

Thickly inhabited area c. 1500, later declined

ENGLAND

IRELAND

FRANCE

PO

ETRURIA

Obsidian

Mycenaean decorative motifs from c.1500

Access to Etruria

SPAIN

Villena

El Argar

Los Millares

Successive cultures (c. 2500) influenced by Crete, Mycenae and perhaps Troy

0   150

Miles

6

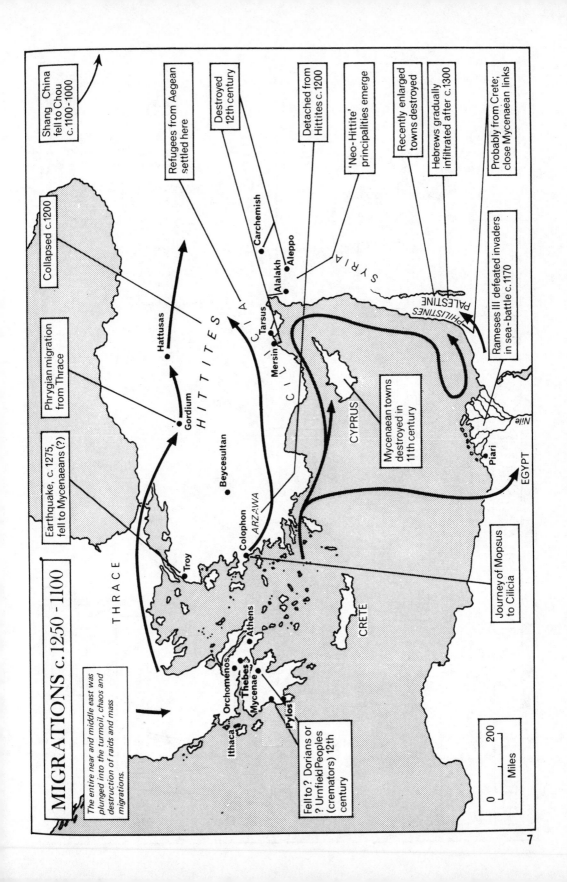

MIGRATIONS c.1250 - 1100

The entire near and middle east was plunged into the turmoil, chaos and destruction of raids and mass migrations.

Shang China fell to Chou c.1100 - 1000

Refugees from Aegean settled here

Destroyed 12th century

Detached from Hittites c.1200

'Neo-Hittite' principalities emerge

Recently enlarged towns destroyed

Hebrews gradually infiltrated after c.1300

Probably from Crete; close Mycenaean links

Rameses III defeated invaders in sea-battle c.1170

Collapsed c.1200

Phrygian migration from Thrace

Earthquake, c.1275, fell to Mycenaeans (?)

Mycenaean towns destroyed in 11th century

Journey of Mopsus to Cilicia

Fell to? Dorians or ? Urnfield Peoples (cremators) 12th century

Carchemish

Aleppo

Alalakh

Tarsus

Mersin

C I L I C I A

Hattusas

H I T T I T E S

Gordium

Beycesultan

Troy

THRACE

Colophon

ARZAWA

CYPRUS

SYRIA

PALESTINE

PHILISTINES

Nile

Piari

EGYPT

CRETE

Athens

Orchomenos

Thebes

Mycenae

Pylos

Ithaca

0   200
Miles

7

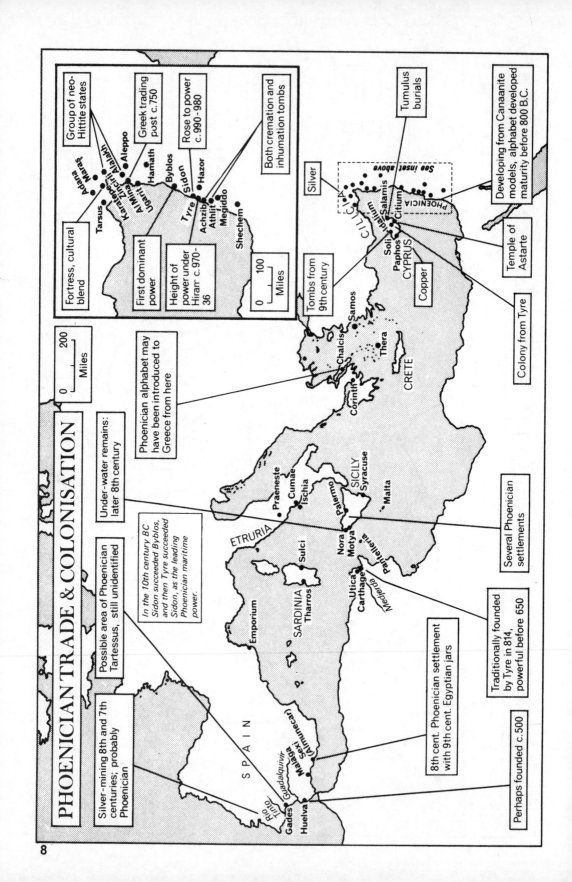

PHOENICIAN TRADE & COLONISATION

Silver-mining 8th and 7th centuries; probably Phoenician

Possible area of Phoenician Tartessus, still unidentified

Under-water remains: later 8th century

Phoenician alphabet may have been introduced to Greece from here

In the 10th century BC Sidon succeeded Byblos, and then Tyre succeeded Sidon, as the leading Phoenician maritime power.

Perhaps founded c. 500

8th cent. Phoenician settlement with 9th cent. Egyptian jars

Traditionally founded by Tyre in 814, powerful before 650

Several Phoenician settlements

Colony from Tyre

Temple of Astarte

Developing from Canaanite models, alphabet developed maturity before 800 B.C.

Tumulus burials

Silver

Copper

Tombs from 9th century

Both cremation and inhumation tombs

Rose to power c. 990–980

Greek trading post c. 750

Group of neo-Hittite states

Height of power under Hiram c. 970–36

First dominant power

Fortress, cultural blend

Inset labels (Levant)

Adana, Maraş, Aleppo, Tarsus, Karatepe, Alalakh, Al Mina, Ugarit, Hamath, Byblos, Sidon, Tyre, Hazor, Achzib, Athlit, Megiddo, Shechem

0 100 Miles

Main map labels

0 200 Miles

SPAIN, Rio Tinto, Guadalquivir, Gades, Malaga, Sexi (Almuñecar), Huelva

SARDINIA, Emporium, Sulci, Tharros, ETRURIA, Praeneste, Cumae, Ischia, Palermo, SICILY, Syracuse, Malta, Nora, Motya, Pantelleria, Utica, Carthage, Medjerda

Chalcis, Samos, Corinth, Thera, CRETE

CILICIA, Soli, Paphos, Salamis, Citium, CYPRUS, PHOENICIA

See inset above

8

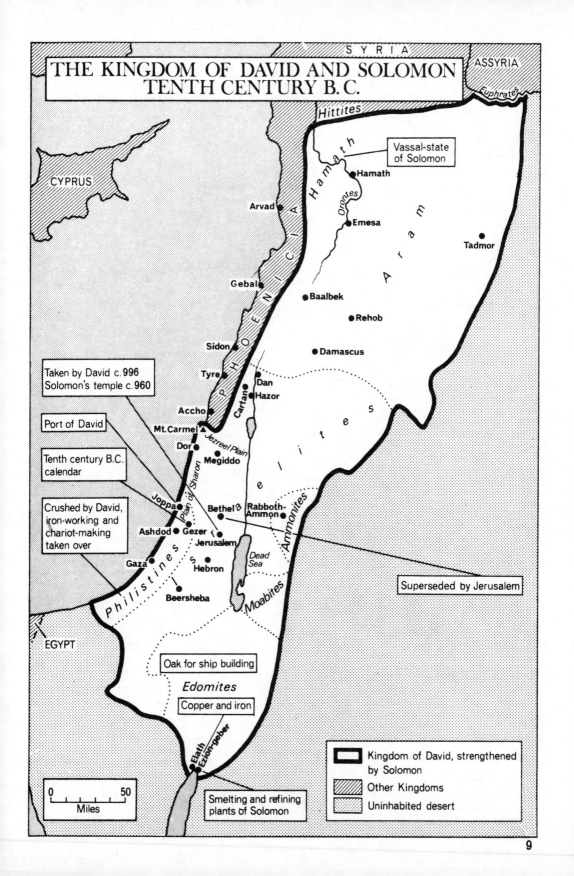

THE KINGDOM OF DAVID AND SOLOMON TENTH CENTURY B.C.

SYRIA

ASSYRIA

Euphrates

CYPRUS

Hittites

Vassal-state of Solomon

Arvad

Hamath

Orontes

Emesa

Tadmor

A
r
a
m

Gebal

Baalbek

Rehob

Sidon

Damascus

Taken by David c.996
Solomon's temple c.960

Tyre

Dan

Hazor

Cartan

Accho

Port of David

Mt.Carmel

Dor

Jezreel Plain

Tenth century B.C.
calendar

Megiddo

I
s
r
a
e
l
i
t
e
s

Plain of Sharon

Crushed by David,
iron-working and
chariot-making
taken over

Joppa

Bethel

Rabboth-
Ammon

Ashdod

Gezer

Jerusalem

A
m
m
o
n
i
t
e
s

P
h
i
l
i
s
t
i
n
e
s

Gaza

Hebron

Dead
Sea

Superseded by Jerusalem

Beersheba

Moabites

EGYPT

Oak for ship building

Edomites

Copper and iron

Elath
Ezion-geber

0	50

Miles

Smelting and refining
plants of Solomon

	Kingdom of David, strengthened by Solomon
	Other Kingdoms
	Uninhabited desert

9

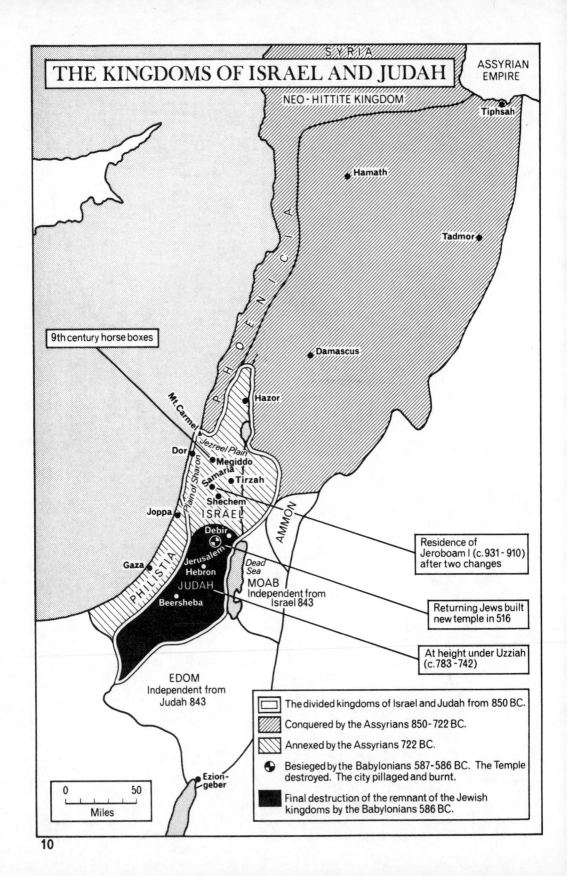

THE KINGDOMS OF ISRAEL AND JUDAH

SYRIA

ASSYRIAN EMPIRE

NEO - HITTITE KINGDOM

Tiphsah

Hamath

Tadmor

9th century horse boxes

P H O E N I C I A

Damascus

Mt. Carmel

Hazor

Jezreel Plain

Dor

Megiddo

Samaria • Tirzah

Plain of Sharon

Shechem

Joppa

ISRAEL

AMMON

Debir

Jerusalem

Gaza

Hebron

Dead Sea

P H I L I S T I A

JUDAH

MOAB
Independent from
Israel 843

Beersheba

Residence of
Jeroboam I (c. 931 - 910)
after two changes

Returning Jews built
new temple in 516

At height under Uzziah
(c. 783 - 742)

EDOM
Independent from
Judah 843

	The divided kingdoms of Israel and Judah from 850 BC.
	Conquered by the Assyrians 850 - 722 BC.
	Annexed by the Assyrians 722 BC.
✪	Besieged by the Babylonians 587 - 586 BC. The Temple destroyed. The city pillaged and burnt.
	Final destruction of the remnant of the Jewish kingdoms by the Babylonians 586 BC.

Ezion-geber

0   50

Miles

10

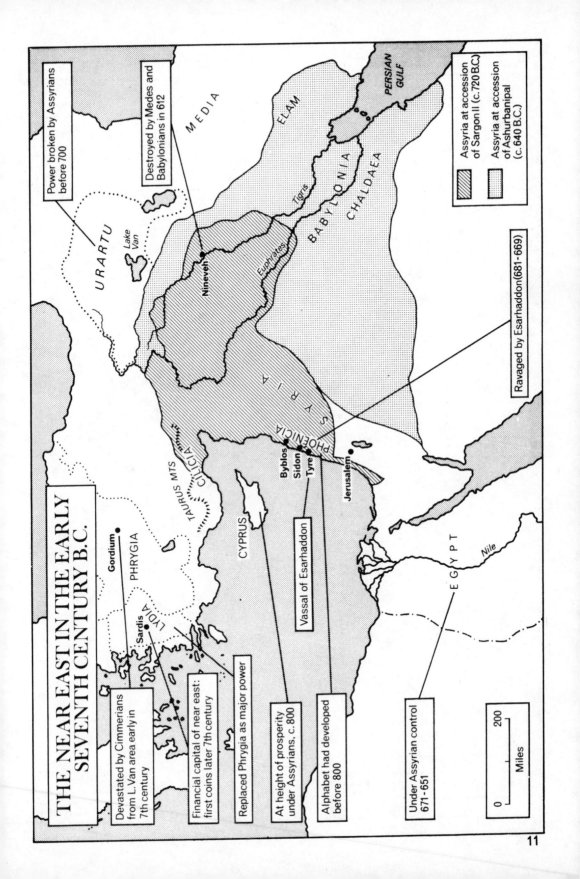

THE NEAR EAST IN THE EARLY
SEVENTH CENTURY B.C.

Assyria at accession of Sargon II (c. 720 B.C.)

Assyria at accession of Ashurbanipal (c. 640 B.C.)

Power broken by Assyrians before 700

Destroyed by Medes and Babylonians in 612

Ravaged by Esarhaddon(681-669)

MEDIA

ELAM

PERSIAN GULF

URARTU

Lake Van

Nineveh

BABYLONIA

CHALDAEA

Tigris

Euphrates

SYRIA

TAURUS MTS

CILICIA

PHOENICIA

Byblos

Sidon

Tyre

Jerusalem

Vassal of Esarhaddon

Devastated by Cimmerians from L. Van area early in 7th century

Financial capital of near east: first coins later 7th century

Replaced Phrygia as major power

At height of prosperity under Assyrians, c. 800

Alphabet had developed before 800

Under Assyrian control 671-651

Gordium

PHRYGIA

Sardis

LYDIA

CYPRUS

EGYPT

Nile

0   200

Miles

11

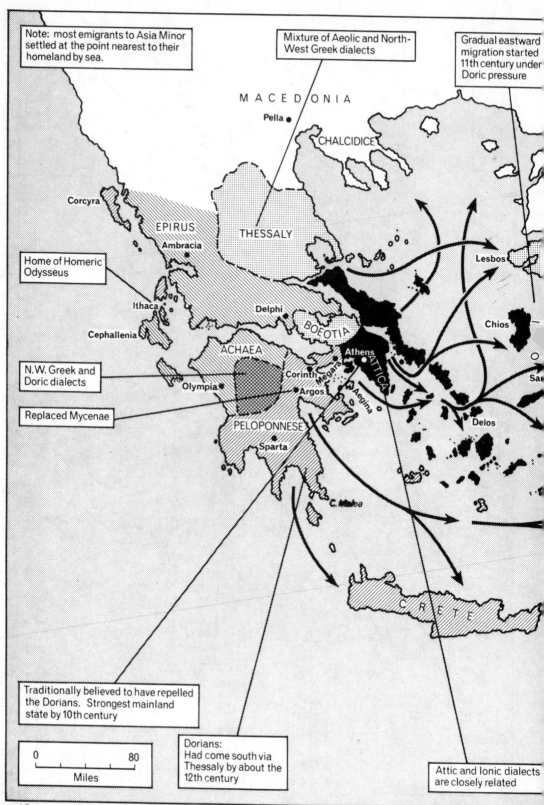

Note: most emigrants to Asia Minor settled at the point nearest to their homeland by sea.

Mixture of Aeolic and North-West Greek dialects

Gradual eastward migration started 11th century under Doric pressure

M A C E D O N I A

Pella ●

CHALCIDICE

Corcyra

EPIRUS

Ambracia

THESSALY

Lesbos

Home of Homeric Odysseus

Ithaca

Delphi

BOEOTIA

Chios

Cephallenia

ACHAEA

Athens
ATTICA

N.W. Greek and Doric dialects

Corinth
Megara

Olympia ●

Argos

Aegina

Sa

Replaced Mycenae

PELOPONNESE

Delos

Sparta

C. Malea

C R E T E

Traditionally believed to have repelled the Dorians. Strongest mainland state by 10th century

0 — 80
Miles

Dorians:
Had come south via Thessaly by about the 12th century

Attic and Ionic dialects are closely related

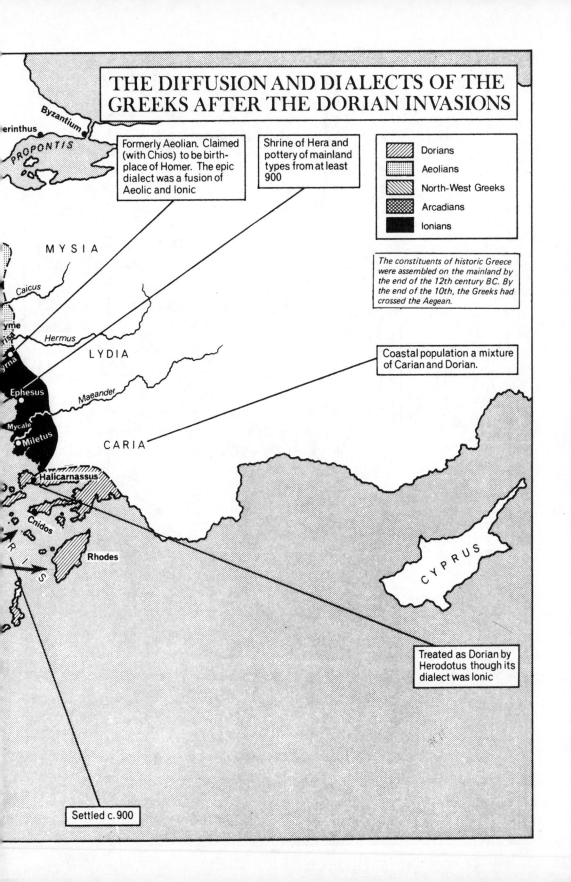

THE DIFFUSION AND DIALECTS OF THE GREEKS AFTER THE DORIAN INVASIONS

Formerly Aeolian. Claimed (with Chios) to be birth-place of Homer. The epic dialect was a fusion of Aeolic and Ionic

Shrine of Hera and pottery of mainland types from at least 900

▨	Dorians
▦	Aeolians
▧	North-West Greeks
▩	Arcadians
■	Ionians

The constituents of historic Greece were assembled on the mainland by the end of the 12th century BC. By the end of the 10th, the Greeks had crossed the Aegean.

Coastal population a mixture of Carian and Dorian.

Treated as Dorian by Herodotus though its dialect was Ionic

Settled c. 900

Byzantium

erinthus

PROPONTIS

MYSIA

Caicus

yme

Hermus

LYDIA

Ephesus

Maeander

Mycale

Miletus

CARIA

Halicarnassus

Cnidos

Rhodes

CYPRUS

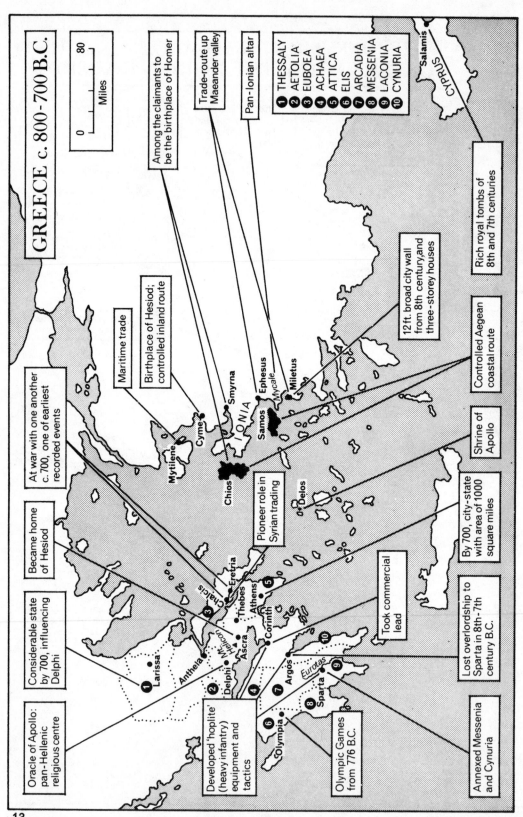

GREECE c. 800-700 B.C.

Miles
0   80

1 THESSALY
2 AETOLIA
3 EUBOEA
4 ACHAEA
5 ATTICA
6 ELIS
7 ARCADIA
8 MESSENIA
9 LACONIA
10 CYNURIA

Among the claimants to be the birthplace of Homer

Trade-route up Maeander valley

Pan-Ionian altar

Maritime trade

Birthplace of Hesiod; controlled inland route

12 ft. broad city wall from 8th century, and three-storey houses

Controlled Aegean coastal route

Rich royal tombs of 8th and 7th centuries

At war with one another c. 700, one of earliest recorded events

Became home of Hesiod

Pioneer role in Syrian trading

Shrine of Apollo

By 700, city-state with area of 1000 square miles

Considerable state by 700, influencing Delphi

Took commercial lead

Lost overlordship to Sparta in 8th-7th century B.C.

Oracle of Apollo: pan-Hellenic religious centre

Developed 'hoplite' (heavy infantry) equipment and tactics

Olympic Games from 776 B.C.

Annexed Messenia and Cynuria

CYPRUS

Salamis

Smyrna
Ephesus
Mycale
Miletus

Mytilene
Cyme
IONIA
Samos
Chios

Delos

Eretria
Chalcis
Thebes
Athens
Corinth

Larissa
Helicon
Anthela
Delphi
Ascra
Argos
Eurotas
Sparta
Olympia

13

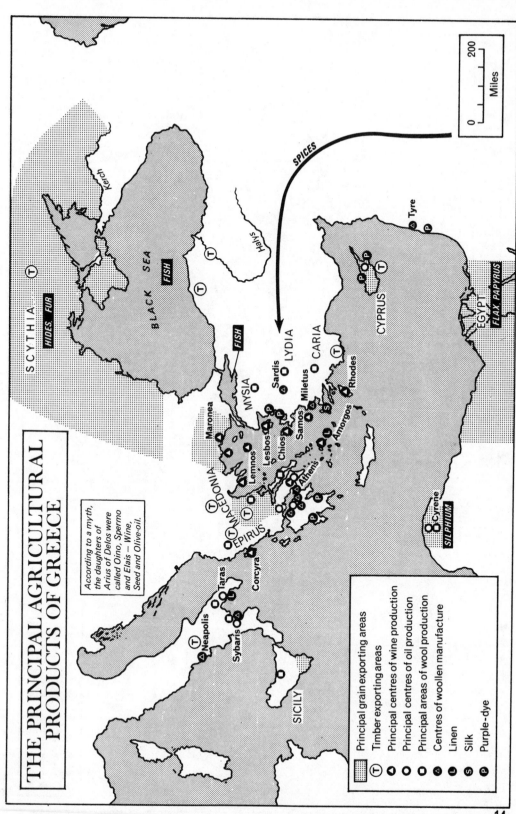

THE PRINCIPAL AGRICULTURAL PRODUCTS OF GREECE

According to a myth, the daughters of Arius of Delos were called Oino, Spermo and Elais – Wine, Seed and Olive-oil.

SCYTHIA
HIDES FUR

Kerch

BLACK SEA
FISH

Halys

SPICES

Tyre

CYPRUS

EGYPT
FLAX PAPYRUS

MYSIA
FISH

Maronea

Lemnos

MACEDONIA

EPIRUS

Sardis
LYDIA

Lesbos
Chios

Samos
Miletus
CARIA

Rhodes

Amorgos

Athens

Cyrene
SILPHIUM

Neapolis

Taras

Sybaris

Corcyra

SICILY

0   200
Miles

Legend

- Principal grain exporting areas
- Principal timber exporting areas
- Principal centres of wine production
- Principal centres of oil production
- Principal areas of wool production
- Centres of woollen manufacture
- Linen
- Silk
- Purple-dye

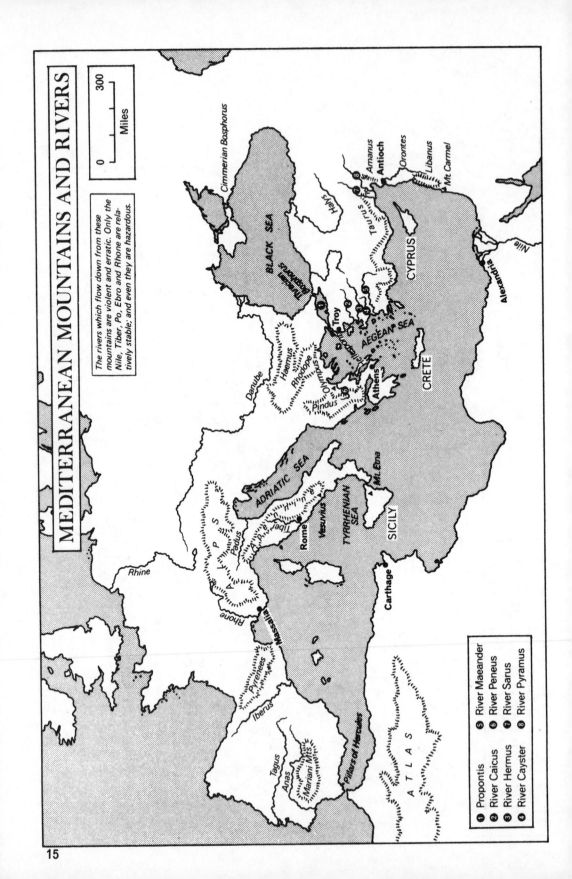

MEDITERRANEAN MOUNTAINS AND RIVERS

0 ——— 300

Miles

The rivers which flow down from these mountains are violent and erratic. Only the Nile, Tiber, Po, Ebro and Rhone are relatively stable, and even they are hazardous.

1. Propontis
2. River Caicus
3. River Hermus
4. River Cayster
5. River Maeander
6. River Peneus
7. River Sarus
8. River Pyramus

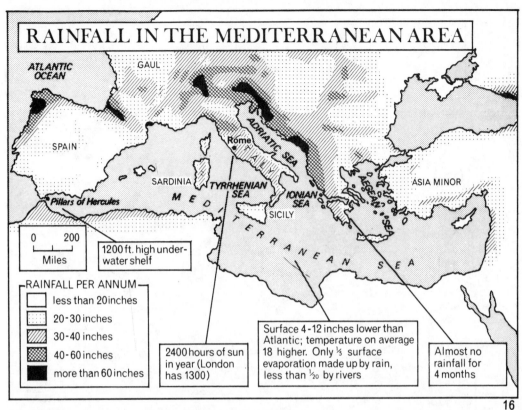

RAINFALL IN THE MEDITERRANEAN AREA

ATLANTIC OCEAN

GAUL

SPAIN

Pillars of Hercules

Rome

ITALY

SARDINIA

TYRRHENIAN SEA

ADRIATIC SEA

IONIAN SEA

SICILY

AEGEAN

ASIA MINOR

M E D I T E R R A N E A N   S E A

0   200
Miles

1200 ft. high under-water shelf

RAINFALL PER ANNUM
less than 20 inches
20 - 30 inches
30 - 40 inches
40 - 60 inches
more than 60 inches

2400 hours of sun in year (London has 1300)

Surface 4 - 12 inches lower than Atlantic; temperature on average 18 higher. Only ⅓ surface evaporation made up by rain, less than ¹⁄₂₀ by rivers

Almost no rainfall for 4 months

16

MINERALS IN THE EASTERN MEDITERRANEAN AREA

■ Gold
□ Silver or ore containing silver
△ Iron
▲ Copper
* Marble

ILLYRIA

ADRIATIC SEA

BLACK   SEA

THRACE

Trapezus

MACEDONIA

ARMENIA

EPIRUS

Dodona

Troy

Hellespont

AEGEAN SEA

Hermus

Ephesus

Maeander

Miletus

ASIA MINOR

Athens

PELOPONNESE

0   200
Miles

CRETE

CYPRUS

17

THE RELIGIOUS CENTRES OF GREECE

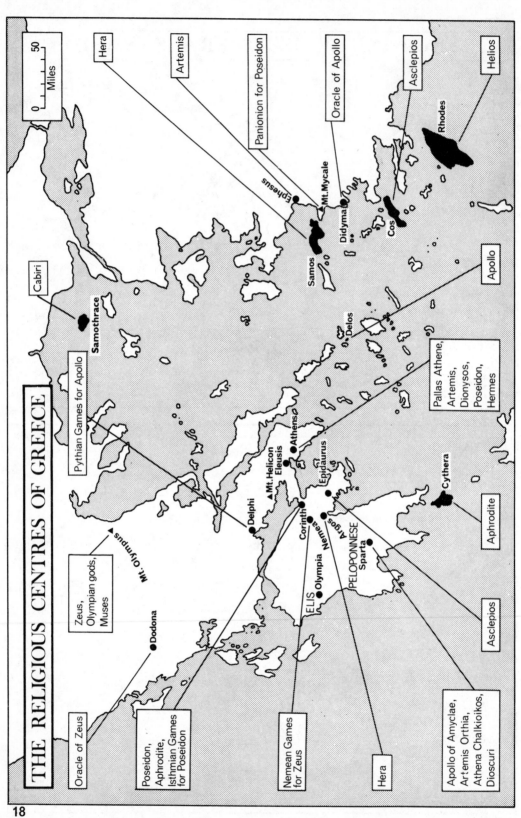

Miles 0 50

Hera

Artemis

Panionion for Poseidon

Oracle of Apollo

Asclepios

Helios

Rhodes

Cabiri

Samothrace

Ephesus

Mt.Mycale

Samos

Didyma

Cos

Apollo

Pythian Games for Apollo

Delos

Pallas Athene, Artemis, Dionysos, Poseidon, Hermes

Oracle of Zeus

Zeus, Olympian gods, Muses

Mt.Olympus

Delphi

Mt.Helicon

Eleusis

Athens

Epidaurus

Cythera

Aphrodite

Dodona

Corinth

Nemea

Argos

ELIS

Olympia

PELOPONNESE

Sparta

Asclepios

Poseidon, Aphrodite, Isthmian Games for Poseidon

Nemean Games for Zeus

Hera

Apollo of Amyclae, Artemis Orthia, Athena Chalkioikos, Dioscuri

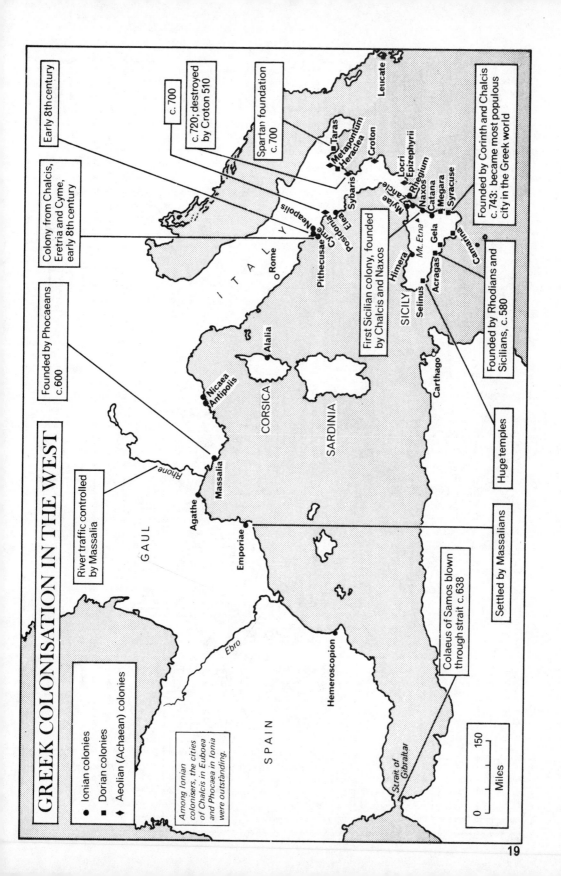

GREEK COLONISATION IN THE WEST

- ● Ionian colonies
- ■ Dorian colonies
- ◆ Aeolian (Achaean) colonies

Among Ionian colonisers, the cities of Chalcis in Euboea and Phocaea in Ionia were outstanding.

Early 8th century

c. 700

c. 720; destroyed by Croton 510

Spartan foundation c. 700

Colony from Chalcis, Eretria and Cyme, early 8th century

First Sicilian colony, founded by Chalcis and Naxos

Founded by Corinth and Chalcis c. 743: became most populous city in the Greek world

Founded by Rhodians and Sicilians, c. 580

Founded by Phocaeans c. 600

River traffic controlled by Massalia

Huge temples

Settled by Massalians

Colaeus of Samos blown through strait c. 638

GAUL

Rhone

Ebro

SPAIN

Strait of Gibraltar

Carthago

CORSICA

SARDINIA

ITALY

SICILY

Mt. Etna

Emporiae

Agathe

Massalia

Nicaea
Antipolis

Alalia

Hemeroscopion

Rome

Pithecusae

Cyme
Neapolis
Posidonia
Elea

Sybaris

Taras
Metapontium
Heraclea

Croton

Leucate

Locri
Epizephyrii
Rhegium
Mylae
Zancle
Naxos
Catana
Megara
Syracuse

Himera

Selinus
Acragas
Gela
Camarina

0   150

Miles

19

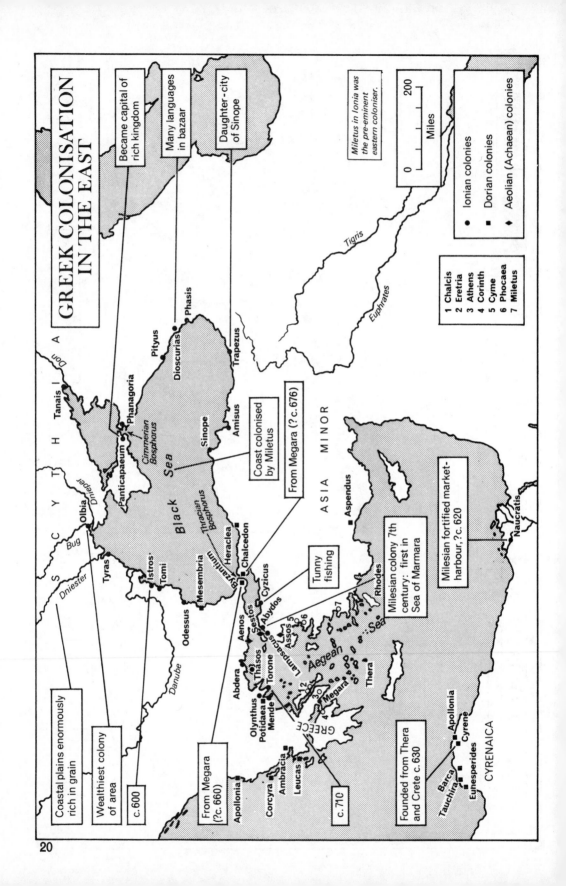

GREEK COLONISATION IN THE EAST

Became capital of rich kingdom

Many languages in bazaar

Daughter-city of Sinope

Miletus in Ionia was the pre-eminent eastern coloniser.

0   200
Miles

0

● Ionian colonies
■ Dorian colonies
◆ Aeolian (Achaean) colonies

1 Chalcis
2 Eretria
3 Athens
4 Corinth
5 Cyme
6 Phocaea
7 Miletus

Tigris

Euphrates

A

Tanais I

Don

Pityus

Dioscurias

Phasis

SCYTH

Phanagoria

Panticapaeum

Cimmerian Bosphorus

Trapezus

Amisus

Sinope

Coast colonised by Miletus

From Megara (? c. 676)

ASIA MINOR

Olbia

Dnieper

Bug

Black Sea

Thracian Bosphorus

Heraclea

Chalcedon

Byzantium

Aspendus

Tyras

Dniester

Istros

Tomi

Mesembria

Odessus

Cyzicus

Abydos

Tunny fishing

Milesian colony 7th century: first in Sea of Marmara

Milesian fortified market-harbour, ? c. 620

Naucratis

Danube

Aenos

Sestos

Assos

Lampsacus

5

6

7

Rhodes

Abdera

Thasos

Torone

1 2

Aegean Sea

Thera

Coastal plains enormously rich in grain

Wealthiest colony of area

c. 600

Olynthus

Potidaea

Mende

3

4

Megara

GREECE

From Megara (? c. 660)

Apollonia

Corcyra

Ambracia

Leucas

c. 710

Founded from Thera and Crete c. 630

Apollonia

Cyrene

Barca

Tauchira

Euesperides

CYRENAICA

20

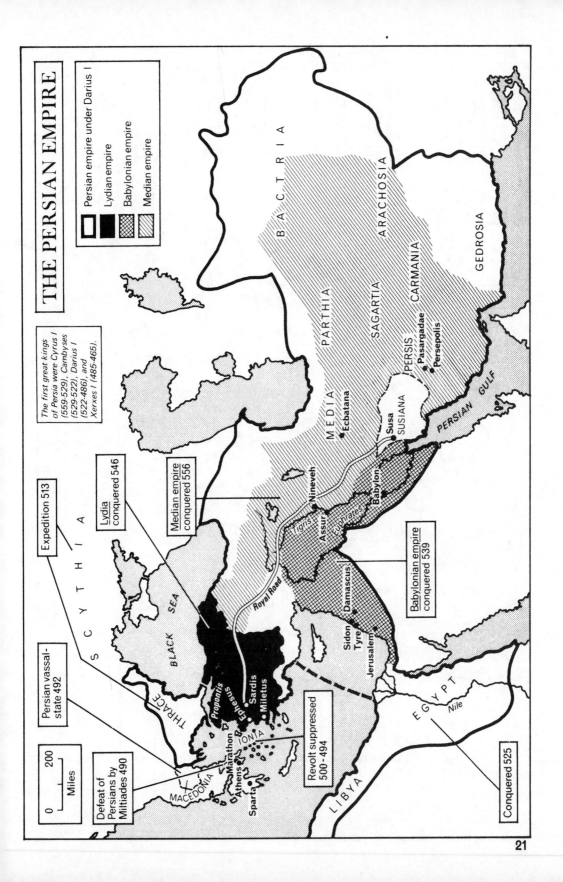

THE PERSIAN EMPIRE

Persian empire under Darius I
Lydian empire
Babylonian empire
Median empire

The first great kings of Persia were Cyrus I (559-529), Cambyses (529-522), Darius I (522-486), and Xerxes I (485-465).

Expedition 513

Persian vassal-state 492

Lydia conquered 546

Median empire conquered 556

Babylonian empire conquered 539

Defeat of Persians by Miltiades 490

Revolt suppressed 500 - 494

Conquered 525

0   200
Miles

SCYTHIA

THRACE

MACEDONIA

BLACK SEA

Propontis

Ephesus
Sardis
Miletus

Marathon
Athens
IONIA
Sparta

LIBYA

EGYPT

Nile

Jerusalem

Sidon
Tyre
Damascus

Assur
Nineveh
Tigris
Euphrates
Babylon

MEDIA
Ecbatana

Susa
SUSIANA

PERSIS
Pasargadae
Persepolis

PERSIAN GULF

Royal Road

BACTRIA

PARTHIA

SAGARTIA

ARACHOSIA

CARMANIA

GEDROSIA

21

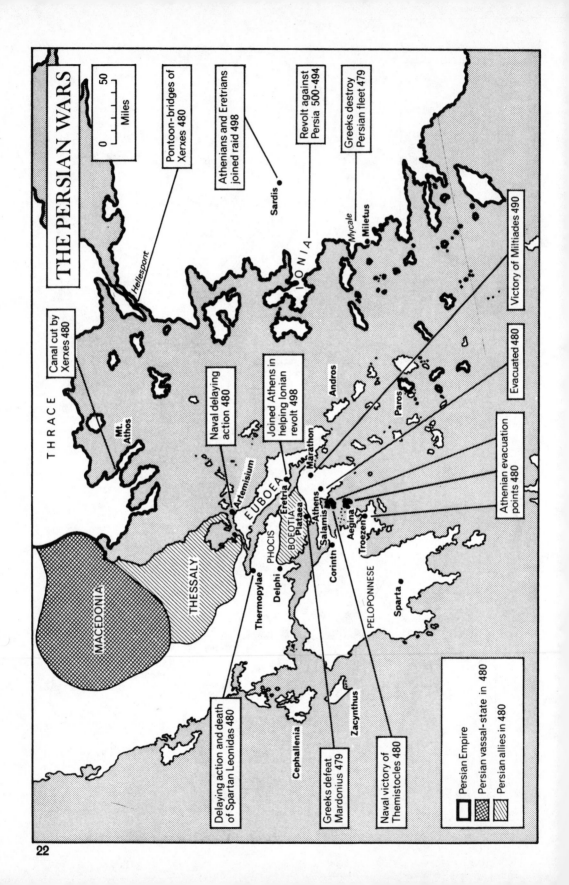

THE PERSIAN WARS

0 — 50 Miles

Pontoon-bridges of Xerxes 480

Athenians and Eretrians joined raid 498

Revolt against Persia 500-494

Greeks destroy Persian fleet 479

Sardis

Mycale
Miletus

IONIA

Canal cut by Xerxes 480

Naval delaying action 480

Joined Athens in helping Ionian revolt 498

Andros

Paros

Victory of Miltiades 490

THRACE

Mt. Athos

Evacuated 480

Artemisium

EUBOEA

Marathon

Athenian evacuation points 480

MACEDONIA

THESSALY

PHOCIS

Thermopylae

Delphi

BOEOTIA
Plataea

Eretria

Athens
Salamis

Aegina
Troezen

Corinth

PELOPONNESE

Sparta

Delaying action and death of Spartan Leonidas 480

Cephallenia

Zacynthus

Greeks defeat Mardonius 479

Naval victory of Themistocles 480

Hellespont

☐ Persian Empire

▦ Persian vassal-state in 480

▨ Persian allies in 480

22

THE BATTLE OF SALAMIS 480 B.C.

N.B. There are also other versions of this battle

The naval victory of the Greeks over the Persians

'But those Greek ships,
Skilfully handled, kept the outer station
Ringing us round and striking in, till ships
Turned turtle, and you could not see the water
For blood and wreckage . . .'
(Aeschylus, The Persians, 417-20, Translated by
A.R. Burn)

Mt. Aegaleos

ELEUSIS

Bay of Eleusis

Mt. Corydallos

PERSIAN LAND ARMY

x Throne of Xerxes

ATHENIAN

SALAMIS

REFUGEES

Cynosura Pt.

PIRAEUS

Cephisus

to Athens

PHALERON

◊ ◊ ◊ Greek fleet

◆ ◆ ◆ Persian fleet

0	1	2

Miles

23

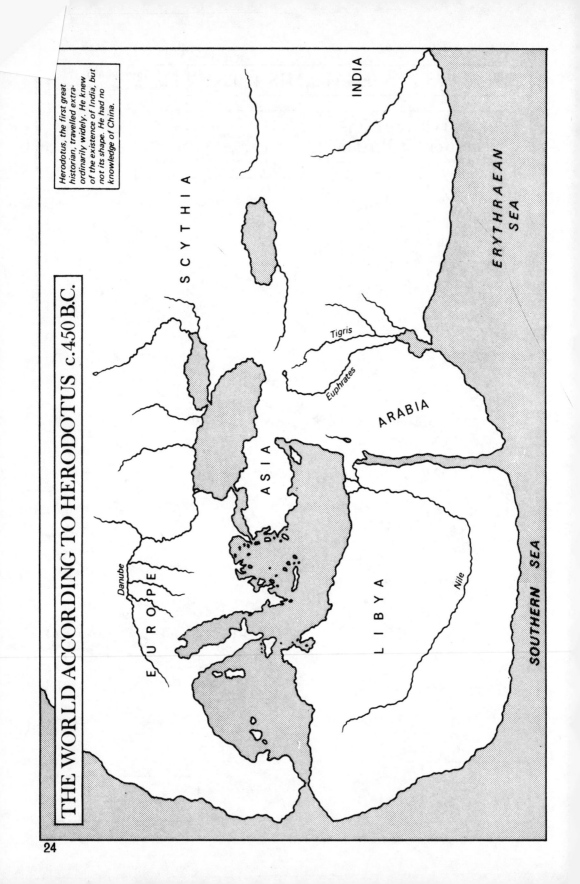

THE WORLD ACCORDING TO HERODOTUS c.450 B.C.

Herodotus, the first great historian, travelled extraordinarily widely. He knew of the existence of India, but not its shape. He had no knowledge of China.

INDIA

SCYTHIA

ERYTHRAEAN SEA

Tigris

Euphrates

ARABIA

ASIA

EUROPE

Danube

LIBYA

Nile

SOUTHERN SEA

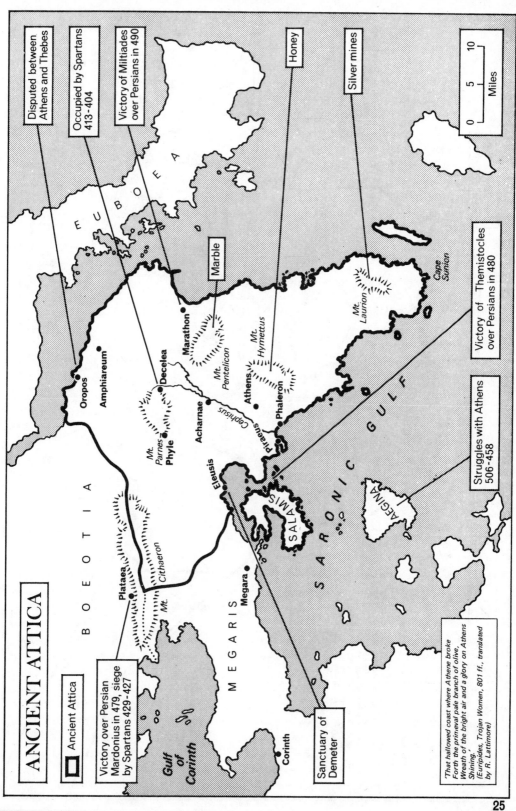

ANCIENT ATTICA

□ Ancient Attica

Disputed between Athens and Thebes

Occupied by Spartans 413-404

Victory of Miltiades over Persians in 490

Honey

Silver mines

Marble

Victory of Themistocles over Persians in 480

Struggles with Athens 506-458

Victory over Persian Mardonius in 479, siege by Spartans 429-427

Sanctuary of Demeter

Miles
0   5   10

EUBOEA

BOEOTIA

Oropos
Amphiareum
Decelea
Marathon
Mt. Pentelicon
Mt. Hymettus
Athens
Phaleron
Cephisus
Acharnae
Mt. Parnes
Phyle
Piraeus
Eleusis
SALAMIS
Mt. Cithaeron
Plataea
MEGARIS
Megara
Corinth
Gulf of Corinth
Cape Sunium
Mt. Laurion
SARONIC GULF
AEGINA

'That hallowed coast where Athene broke
Forth the primeval pale branch of olive,
Wreath of the bright air and a glory on Athens
Shining.'
(Euripides, Trojan Women, 801 ff., translated
by R. Lattimore)

25

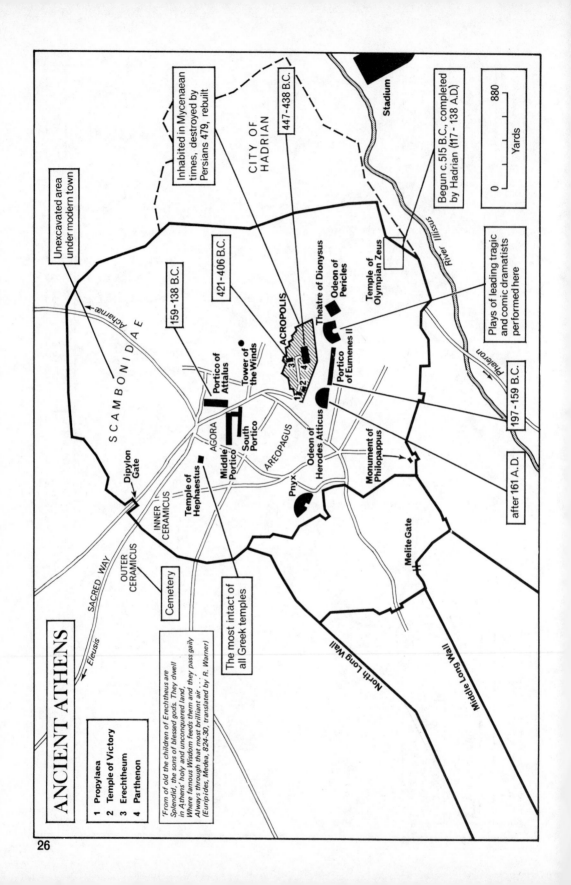

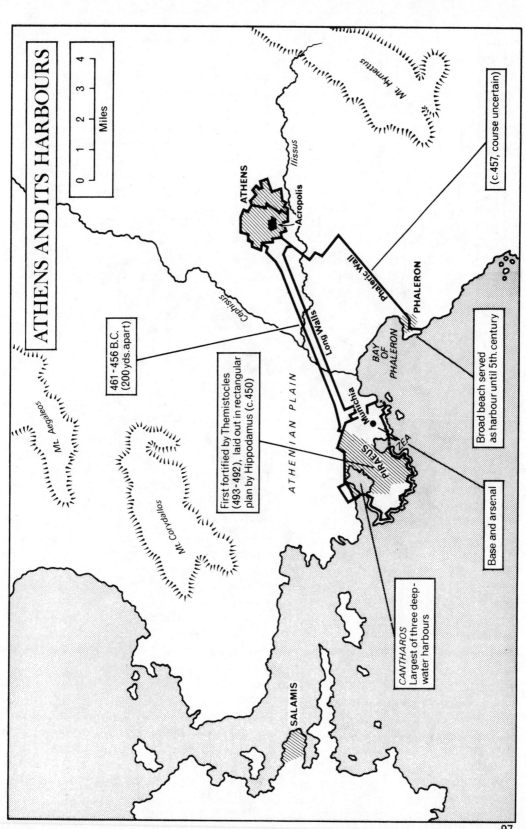

ATHENS AND ITS HARBOURS

Miles
0 1 2 3 4

Mt. Aegaleos

Cephisus

Mt. Corydallos

ATHENIAN PLAIN

ATHENS

Acropolis

Ilissus

Mt. Hymettus

Long Walls

Phaleric Wall

PHALERON

BAY OF PHALERON

Munichia

PIRAEUS

ZEA

SALAMIS

461 - 456 B.C.
(200 yds. apart)

First fortified by Themistocles
(493 - 492), laid out in rectangular
plan by Hippodamus (c. 450)

(c. 457, course uncertain)

Broad beach served
as harbour until 5th. century

Base and arsenal

CANTHAROS
Largest of three deep-
water harbours

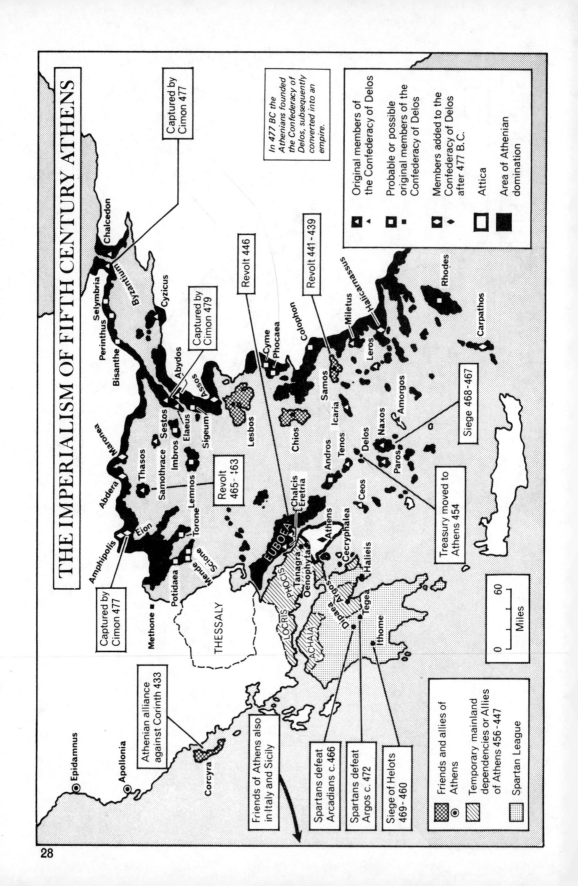

THE IMPERIALISM OF FIFTH CENTURY ATHENS

In 477 BC the Athenians founded the Confederacy of Delos, subsequently converted into an empire.

Original members of the Confederacy of Delos

Probable or possible original members of the Confederacy of Delos

Members added to the Confederacy of Delos after 477 B.C.

Attica

Area of Athenian domination

Captured by Cimon 477

Captured by Cimon 479

Revolt 446

Revolt 441 - 439

Captured by Cimon 477

Revolt 465 - 463

Treasury moved to Athens 454

Siege 468 - 467

Athenian alliance against Corinth 433

Friends of Athens also in Italy and Sicily

Spartans defeat Arcadians c. 466

Spartans defeat Argos c. 472

Siege of Helots 469 - 460

Friends and allies of Athens

Temporary mainland dependencies or Allies of Athens 456 - 447

Spartan League

Chalcedon
Selymbria
Perinthus
Byzantium
Bisanthe
Cyzicus
Abydos
Assos
Sestos
Elaeus
Sigeum
Imbros
Samothrace
Lemnos
Thasos
Abdera
Torone
Maroneia
Eion
Amphipolis
Methone
Potidaea
Mende
Scione
Cyme
Phocaea
Colophon
Miletus
Halicarnassus
Leros
Rhodes
Carpathos
Samos
Icaria
Lesbos
Chios
Andros
Tenos
Delos
Naxos
Amorgos
Paros
Ceos
Chalcis
Eretria
EUBOEA
PHOCIS
LOCRIS
Tanagra
Oenophyta
Athens
Cecryphalea
Halieis
ARGOS
Dipaea
Tegea
Ithome
ACHAIA
THESSALY
Corcyra
Epidamnus
Apollonia

0   60
Miles

28

GREECE IN THE PELOPONNESIAN WAR 431-404 B.C.

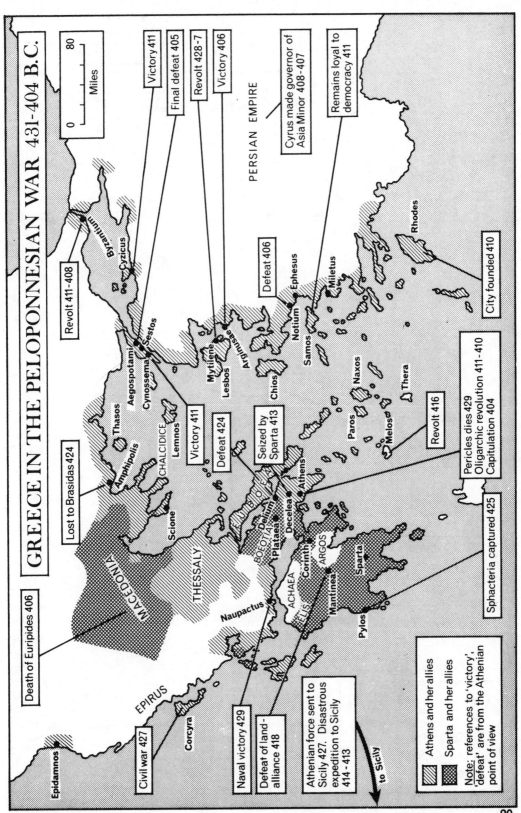

0 — 80
Miles

Victory 411
Final defeat 405
Revolt 428-7
Victory 406

PERSIAN EMPIRE

Cyrus made governor of Asia Minor 408-407

Remains loyal to democracy 411

Revolt 411-408

Byzantium

Cyzicus

Rhodes

Defeat 406

Ephesus

Miletus

City founded 410

Aegospotami

Cynossema

Sestos

Thasos

CHALCIDICE

Lemnos

Mytilene

Lesbos

Arginusae

Samos

Chios

Victory 411

Defeat 424

Seized by Sparta 413

Amphipolis

Naxos

Paros

Thera

Lost to Brasidas 424

MACEDONIA

Scione

THESSALY

BOEOTIA

Delium

Plataea

Decelea

Athens

Melos

Revolt 416

Pericles dies 429
Oligarchic revolution 411-410
Capitulation 404

Corinth

ARGOS

ACHAEA

ELIS

Mantinea

Sparta

Death of Euripides 406

Sphacteria captured 425

Pylos

EPIRUS

Naupactus

Civil war 427

Naval victory 429

Defeat of land-alliance 418

Athenian force sent to Sicily 427. Disastrous expedition to Sicily 414-413

Corcyra

Epidamnos

to Sicily

Athens and her allies

Sparta and her allies

Note: references to 'victory', 'defeat' are from the Athenian point of view

29

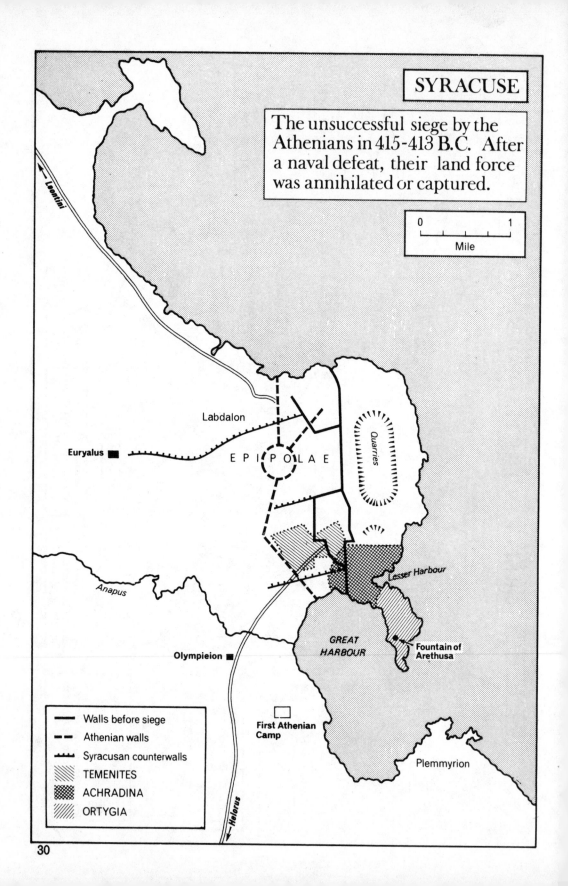

SYRACUSE

The unsuccessful siege by the Athenians in 415-413 B.C. After a naval defeat, their land force was annihilated or captured.

0   1
Mile

Leontini

Labdalon

Euryalus ■

E P I P O L A E

Quarries

Lesser Harbour

Anapus

Olympieion ■

GREAT HARBOUR

Fountain of Arethusa

First Athenian Camp

Plemmyrion

Helorus

— Walls before siege
-- Athenian walls
+++ Syracusan counterwalls
▨ TEMENITES
▓ ACHRADINA
▨ ORTYGIA

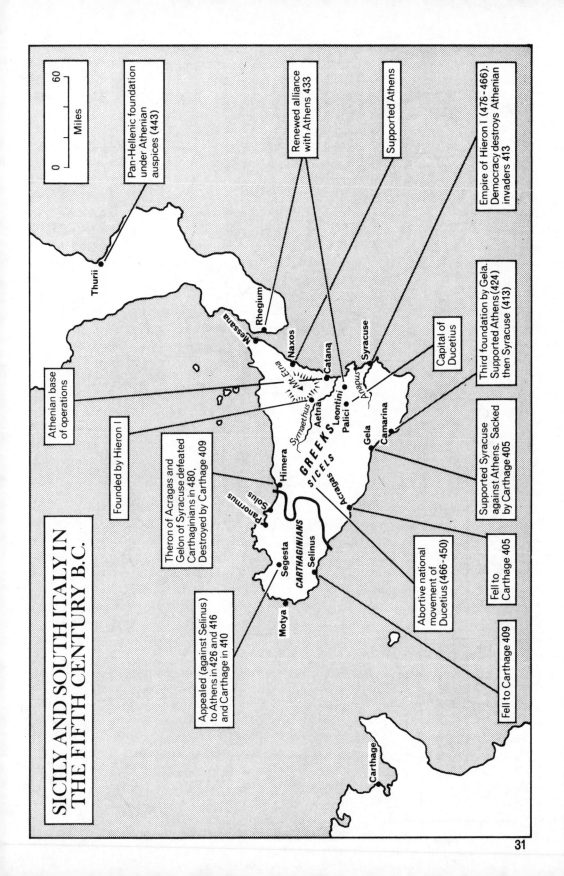

SICILY AND SOUTH ITALY IN THE FIFTH CENTURY B.C.

0   60

Miles

Pan-Hellenic foundation under Athenian auspices (443)

Renewed alliance with Athens 433

Supported Athens

Empire of Hieron I (478 - 466). Democracy destroys Athenian invaders 413

Athenian base of operations

Founded by Hieron I

Theron of Acragas and Gelon of Syracuse defeated Carthaginians in 480. Destroyed by Carthage 409

Capital of Ducetius

Third foundation by Gela. Supported Athens (424) then Syracuse (413)

Supported Syracuse against Athens. Sacked by Carthage 405

Abortive national movement of Ducetius (466 - 450)

Fell to Carthage 405

Appealed (against Selinus) to Athens in 426 and 416 and Carthage in 410

Fell to Carthage 409

Thurii

Rhegium

Messana

Naxos

Catana

Mt. Etna

Syracuse

Symaethus

Aetna

Leontini

Anapus

Palici

GREEKS

SICELS

Gela

Camarina

Himera

Acragas

Solus

Panormus

Segesta

Selinus

CARTHAGINIANS

Motya

Carthage

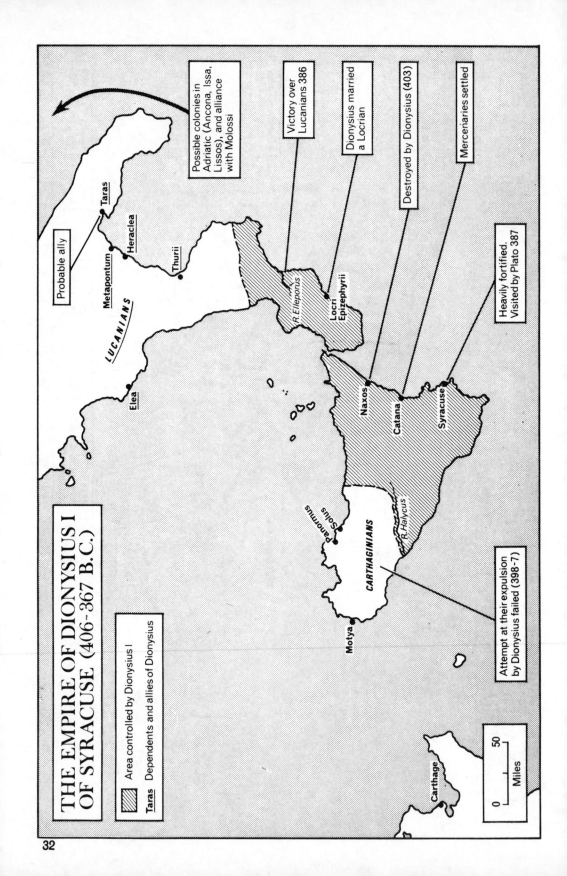

THE EMPIRE OF DIONYSIUS I OF SYRACUSE (406–367 B.C.)

Area controlled by Dionysius I

Taras Dependents and allies of Dionysius

Probable ally

Possible colonies in Adriatic (Ancona, Issa, Lissos), and alliance with Molossi

Victory over Lucanians 386

Dionysius married a Locrian

Destroyed by Dionysius (403)

Mercenaries settled

Heavily fortified. Visited by Plato 387

Attempt at their expulsion by Dionysius failed (398-7)

Taras

Metapontum

Heraclea

Thurii

LUCANIANS

Elea

R. Elleporus

Locri Epizephyrii

Naxos

Catana

Syracuse

Solus

Panormus

R. Halycus

CARTHAGINIANS

Motya

Carthage

0   50
Miles

32

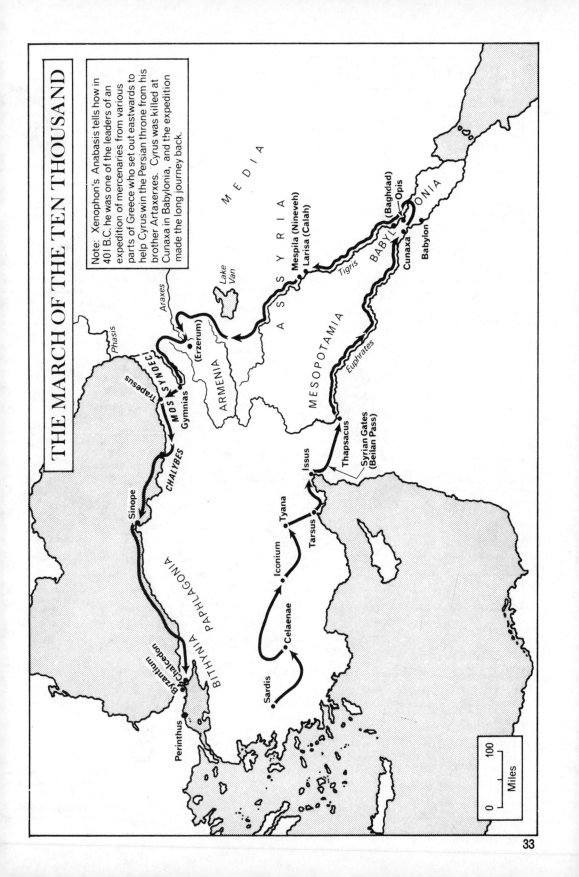

THE MARCH OF THE TEN THOUSAND

Note: Xenophon's *Anabasis* tells how in 401 B.C. he was one of the leaders of an expedition of mercenaries from various parts of Greece who set out eastwards to help Cyrus win the Persian throne from his brother Artaxerxes. Cyrus was killed at Cunaxa in Babylonia, and the expedition made the long journey back.

MEDIA

ASSYRIA

Mespila (Nineveh)
Larisa (Calah)

Tigris

Lake Van

Araxes

Phasis

(Erzerum)

ARMENIA

MESOPOTAMIA

Euphrates

BABYL ONIA

(Baghdad)
Opis

Cunaxa

Babylon

MOSSYNOECI

Trapesus

Gymnias

CHALYBES

Sinope

Thapsacus

Syrian Gates
(Beilan Pass)

Issus

Tyana

Tarsus

Iconium

Celaenae

PAPHLAGONIA

BITHYNIA

Sardis

Byzantium
Chalcedon

Perinthus

100

Miles

0

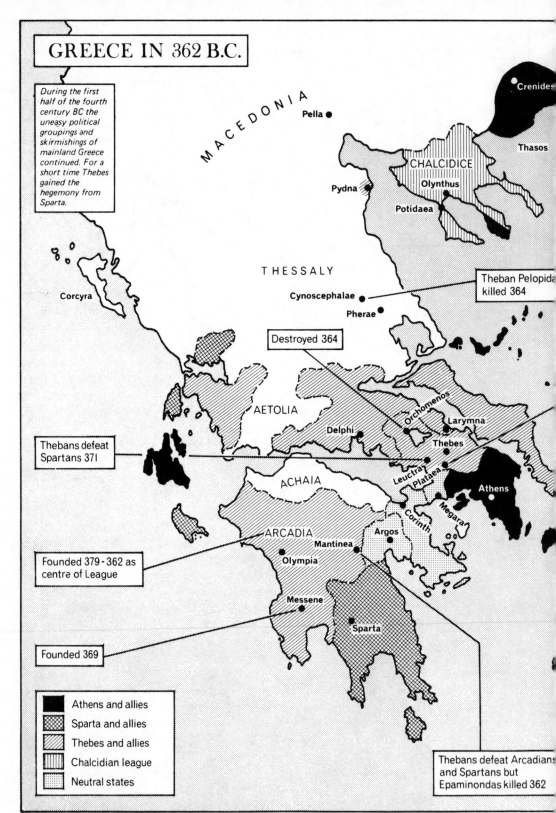

GREECE IN 362 B.C.

During the first half of the fourth century BC the uneasy political groupings and skirmishings of mainland Greece continued. For a short time Thebes gained the hegemony from Sparta.

MACEDONIA

Crenides

Pella

Thasos

CHALCIDICE

Olynthus

Pydna

Potidaea

THESSALY

Corcyra

Cynoscephalae

Theban Pelopida[s]
killed 364

Pherae

Destroyed 364

AETOLIA

Orchomenos

Larymna

Delphi

Thebes

Thebans defeat
Spartans 371

Leuctra

Plataea

Athens

ACHAIA

Corinth

Megara

ARCADIA

Argos

Mantinea

Founded 379 - 362 as
centre of League

Olympia

Founded 369

Messene

Sparta

Athens and allies

Sparta and allies

Thebes and allies

Chalcidian league

Neutral states

Thebans defeat Arcadian[s]
and Spartans but
Epaminondas killed 362

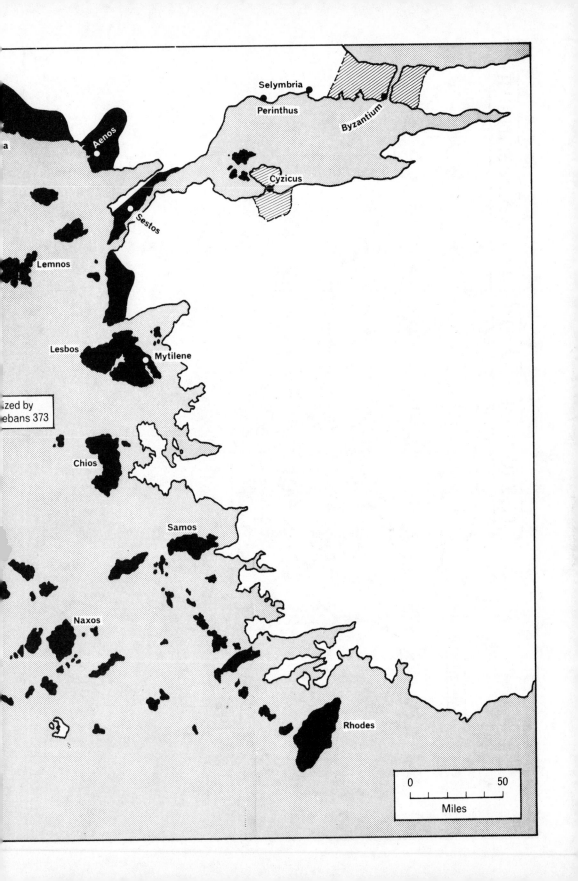

Selymbria

Perinthus

Byzantium

Aenos

Cyzicus

Sestos

Lemnos

Lesbos

Mytilene

...zed by
...ebans 373

Chios

Samos

Naxos

Rhodes

0				50

Miles

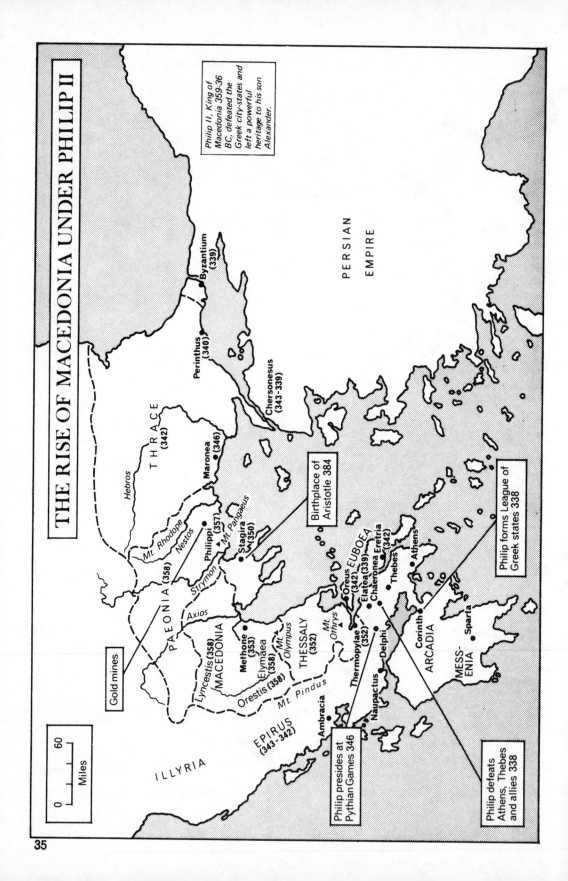

THE RISE OF MACEDONIA UNDER PHILIP II

Philip II, King of Macedonia 359-36 BC, defeated the Greek city-states and left a powerful heritage to his son Alexander.

PERSIAN EMPIRE

Byzantium (339)

Perinthus (340)

Chersonesus (343-339)

THRACE (342)

Maronea (346)

Hebros

Mt. Rhodope

Nestos

Philippi (357)

Mt. Pangaeus

Stagira (350)

Birthplace of Aristotle 384

PAEONIA (358)

Strymon

Axios

EUBOEA

Oreus (342)

Elatea (339)

Chaeronea Eretria (342)

Thebes

Athens

Philip forms League of Greek states 338

Gold mines

MACEDONIA

Methone (353)

Elymaea

Orestis (358)

Lyncestis (358)

Elymaea (358)

Mt. Olympus

Mt. Othrys

THESSALY (352)

Thermopylae (352)

Delphi

Corinth

ARCADIA

Sparta

MESS-ENIA

Philip presides at Pythian Games 346

Mt. Pindus

Ambracia

Naupactus

EPIRUS (343-342)

ILLYRIA

Philip defeats Athens, Thebes and allies 338

0   60
Miles

35

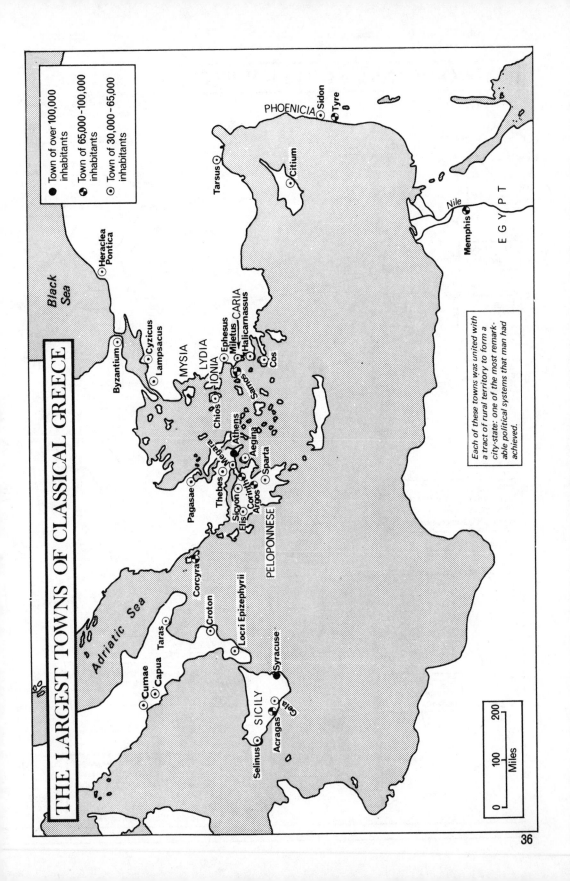

THE LARGEST TOWNS OF CLASSICAL GREECE

Legend:
- ● Town of over 100,000 inhabitants
- ◉ Town of 65,000 -100,000 inhabitants
- ⊙ Town of 30,000 - 65,000 inhabitants

Each of these towns was united with a tract of rural territory to form a city-state: one of the most remarkable political systems that man had achieved.

Black Sea

Adriatic Sea

PHOENICIA
Sidon
Tyre
Tarsus
Citium
Nile
Memphis
EGYPT

Heraclea Pontica
Byzantium
Cyzicus
Lampsacus
MYSIA
LYDIA
IONIA
Ephesus
Miletus CARIA
Halicarnassus
Cos
Samos
Chios
Athens
Megara
Aegina
Sparta
Thebes
Sicyon
Elis
Corinth
Argos
PELOPONNESE
Pagasae

Corcyra
Croton
Locri Epizephyrii
Taras
Capua
Cumae
Syracuse
Gela
SICILY
Acragas
Selinus

0   100   200
Miles

36

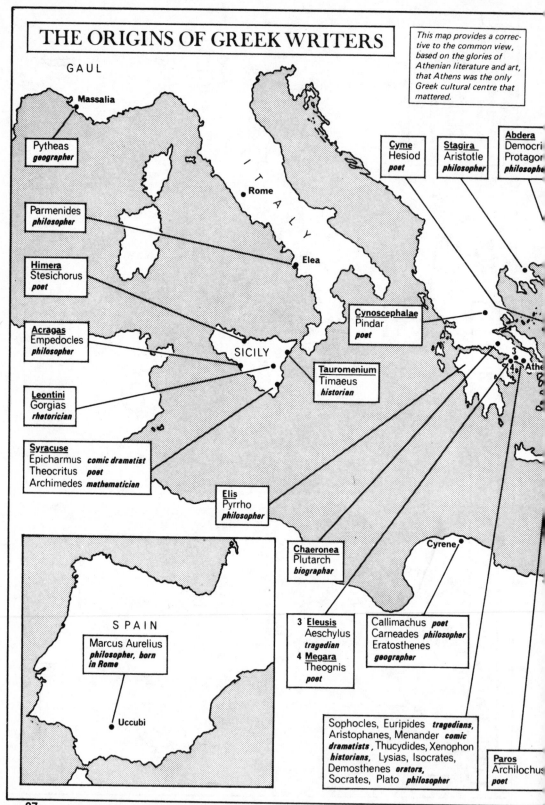

THE ORIGINS OF GREEK WRITERS

This map provides a corrective to the common view, based on the glories of Athenian literature and art, that Athens was the only Greek cultural centre that mattered.

GAUL

Massalia

Pytheas
geographer

Parmenides
philosopher

Himera
Stesichorus
poet

Acragas
Empedocles
philosopher

Leontini
Gorgias
rhetorician

Syracuse
Epicharmus *comic dramatist*
Theocritus *poet*
Archimedes *mathematician*

Cyme
Hesiod
poet

Stagira
Aristotle
philosopher

Abdera
Democri
Protagon
philosophe

Rome

I T A L Y

Elea

Cynoscephalae
Pindar
poet

SICILY

Tauromenium
Timaeus
historian

3

4   Ath

Elis
Pyrrho
philosopher

Chaeronea
Plutarch
biographer

Cyrene

SPAIN

Marcus Aurelius
philosopher, born in Rome

Uccubi

3 **Eleusis**
Aeschylus
tragedian
4 **Megara**
Theognis
poet

Callimachus *poet*
Carneades *philosopher*
Eratosthenes
geographer

Sophocles, Euripides *tragedians*,
Aristophanes, Menander *comic dramatists*, Thucydides, Xenophon
historians, Lysias, Isocrates,
Demosthenes *orators*,
Socrates, Plato *philosopher*

Paros
Archilochus
poet

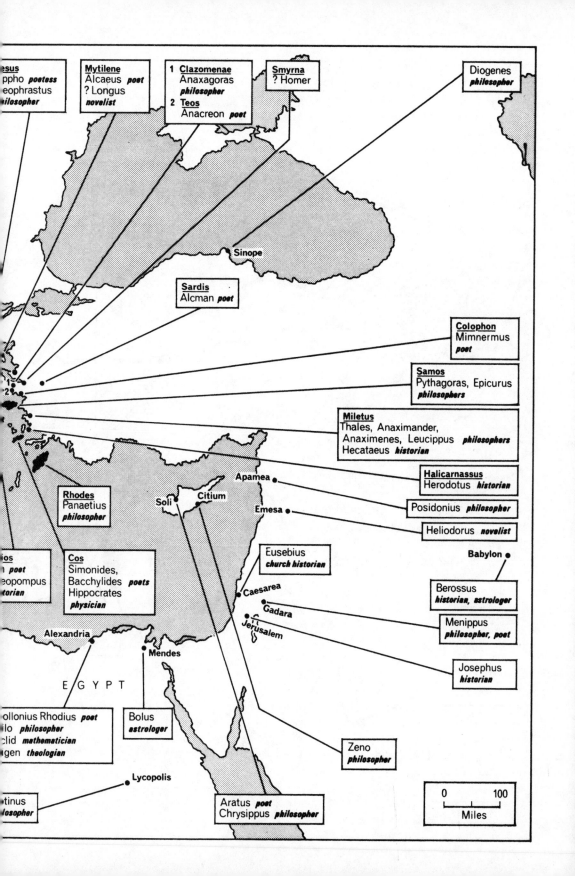

...esus
...ppho *poetess*
...eophrastus
...ilosopher

Mytilene
Alcaeus *poet*
? Longus
novelist

1 **Clazomenae**
Anaxagoras
philosopher
2 **Teos**
Anacreon *poet*

Smyrna
? Homer

Diogenes
philosopher

Sinope

Sardis
Alcman *poet*

Colophon
Mimnermus
poet

Samos
Pythagoras, Epicurus
philosophers

Miletus
Thales, Anaximander,
Anaximenes, Leucippus *philosophers*
Hecataeus *historian*

Apamea

Halicarnassus
Herodotus *historian*

Rhodes
Panaetius
philosopher

Soli **Citium**

Emesa

Posidonius *philosopher*

Heliodorus *novelist*

Babylon

...ios
...n *poet*
...eopompus
...torian

Cos
Simonides,
Bacchylides *poets*
Hippocrates
physician

Eusebius
church historian

Berossus
historian, astrologer

Caesarea

Gadara

Alexandria

Mendes

Jerusalem

Menippus
philosopher, poet

Josephus
historian

E G Y P T

...ollonius Rhodius *poet*
...ilo *philosopher*
...clid *mathematician*
...gen *theologian*

Bolus
astrologer

Zeno
philosopher

Lycopolis

...tinus
...losopher

Aratus *poet*
Chrysippus *philosopher*

0   100
Miles

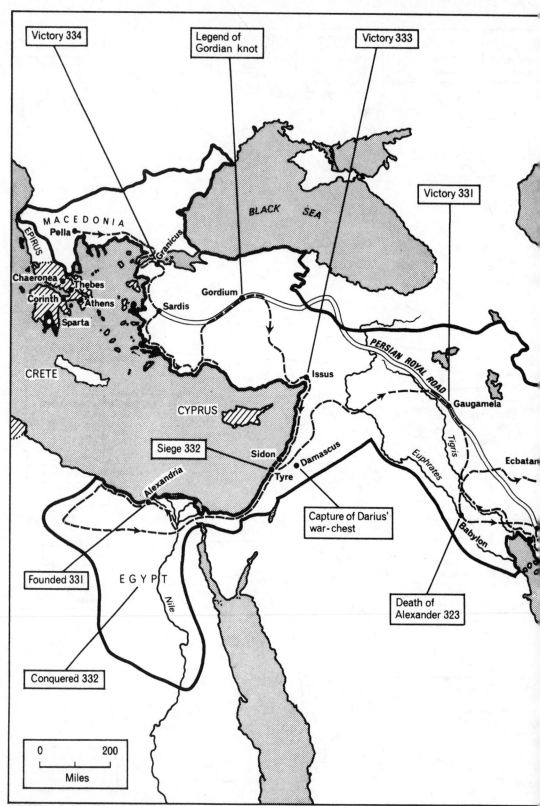

Victory 334

Legend of
Gordian knot

Victory 333

Victory 331

MACEDONIA

EPIRUS

Pella

BLACK   SEA

Chaeronea

Thebes

Corinth

Athens

Sparta

Sardis

Gordium

Granicus

CRETE

CYPRUS

Issus

PERSIAN ROYAL ROAD

Gaugamela

Tigris

Euphrates

Ecbatan

Siege 332

Sidon

Tyre

Damascus

Alexandria

Capture of Darius'
war-chest

Babylon

Founded 331

EGYPT

Nile

Death of
Alexander 323

Conquered 332

0   200

Miles

THE CONQUESTS OF ALEXANDER THE GREAT

Alexander III of Macedonia succeed-ed his father Philip II in 336, and, after conquests that utterly changed the world, died at Babylon in 323.

	Empire of Alexander the Great
	Dependent states
▓	Independent states
--→	Routes of Alexander the Great

Conquered 328

Darius murdered 330

CASPIAN SEA

SOGDIANA

Alexandria Eschate

PUNJAB

Alexandria (Merv)

Bactra (Balkh)

BACTRIA

Alexandria

Taxila

Bucephala

Damghan

PARTHIA

Alexandria (Herat)

Alexandria (Ghazni)

Indus

Hydaspes

Occupied 331

Alexandria (Kandahar)

Alexandria

Persepolis

GEDROSIA

PERSIAN GULF

Victory over Indian king Porus 326

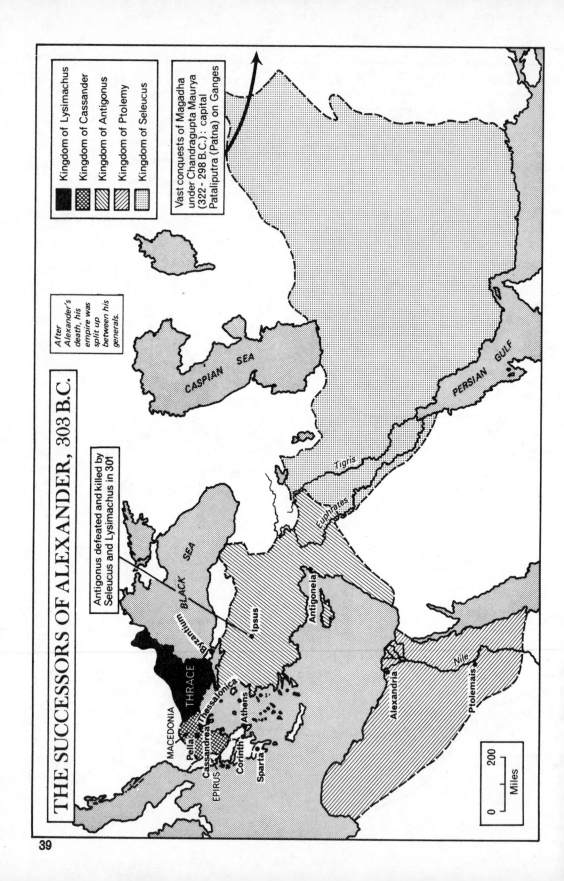

THE SUCCESSORS OF ALEXANDER, 303 B.C.

After Alexander's death, his empire was split up between his generals.

Vast conquests of Magadha under Chandragupta Maurya (322 - 298 B.C.): capital Pataliputra (Patna) on Ganges

Kingdom of Lysimachus
Kingdom of Cassander
Kingdom of Antigonus
Kingdom of Ptolemy
Kingdom of Seleucus

Antigonus defeated and killed by Seleucus and Lysimachus in 301

CASPIAN SEA

BLACK SEA

Byzantium

THRACE

MACEDONIA

Pella

Cassandrea

Thessalonica

EPIRUS

Athens

Corinth

Sparta

Ipsus

Antigoneia

Tigris

Euphrates

PERSIAN GULF

Nile

Alexandria

Ptolemais

0   200

Miles

39

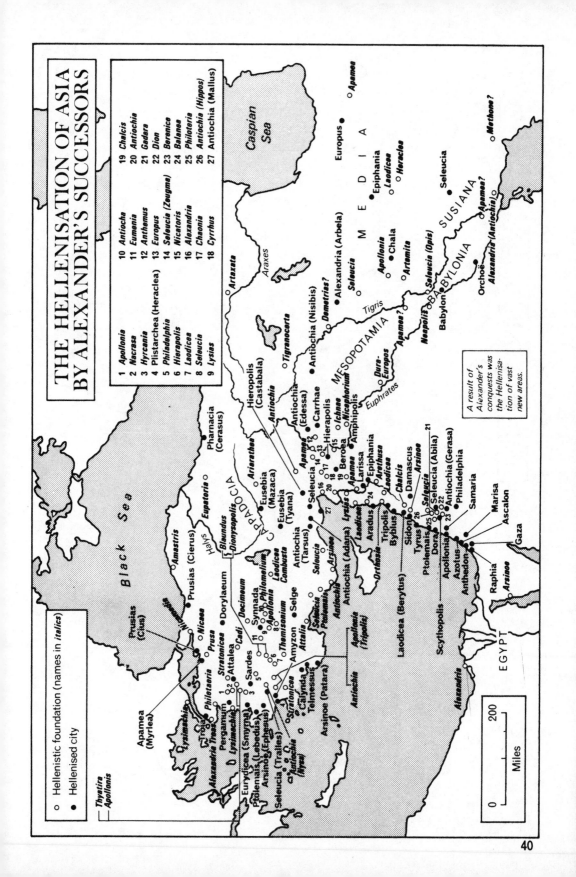

THE HELLENISATION OF ASIA BY ALEXANDER'S SUCCESSORS

1 *Apollonia*	10 *Antiocha*	19 *Chalcis*	
2 *Nacrasa*	11 *Eumenia*	20 *Antiochia*	
3 *Hyrcania*	12 *Anthemus*	21 *Gadara*	
4 *Plistarchea (Heraclea)*	13 *Europus*	22 *Dion*	
5 *Philadelphia*	14 *Seleucia (Zeugma)*	23 *Berenice*	
6 *Hierapolis*	15 *Nicatoris*	24 *Balanea*	
7 *Laodicea*	16 *Alexandria*	25 *Philoteria*	
8 *Seleucia*	17 *Chaonia*	26 *Antiochia (Hippos)*	
9 *Lysias*	18 *Cyrrhus*	27 *Antiochia (Mallus)*	

A result of Alexander's conquests was the Hellenisation of vast new areas.

○ Hellenistic foundation (names in *italics*)
● Hellenised city

Thyatira
Apollonis

Miles
0   200

40

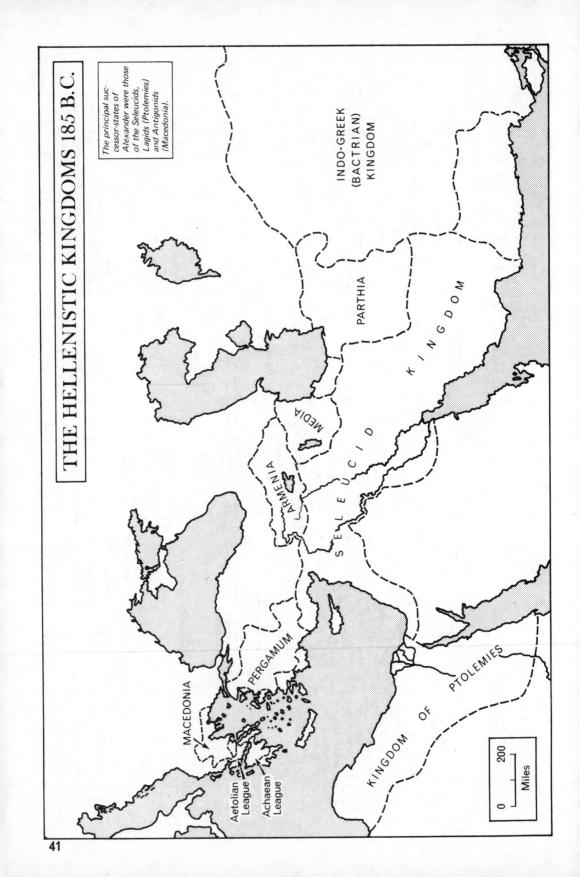

THE HELLENISTIC KINGDOMS 185 B.C.

The principal successor-states of Alexander were those of the Seleucids, Lagids (Ptolemies) and Antigonids (Macedonia).

INDO-GREEK (BACTRIAN) KINGDOM

PARTHIA

MEDIA

ARMENIA

SELEUCID KINGDOM

PERGAMUM

MACEDONIA

Aetolian League

Achaean League

KINGDOM OF PTOLEMIES

0   200
Miles

41

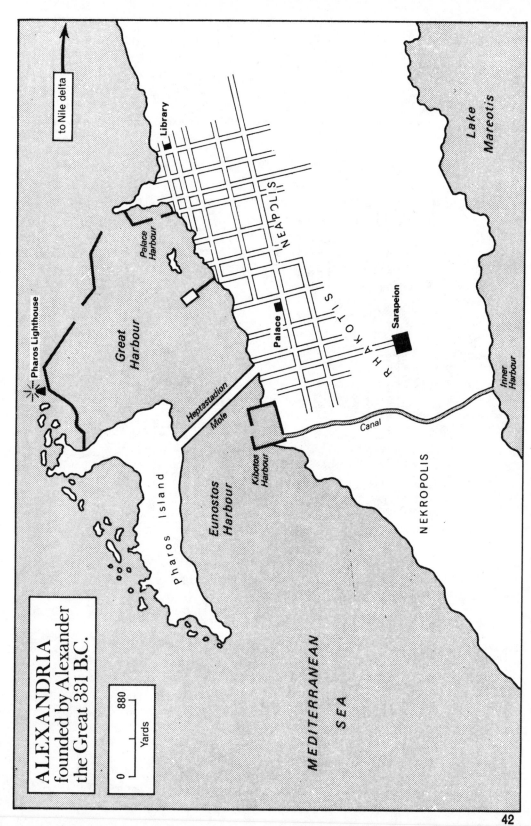

ALEXANDRIA
founded by Alexander
the Great 331 B.C.

0   880
Yards

to Nile delta

Library

Palace
Harbour

Pharos Lighthouse

Great
Harbour

NEAPOLIS

Palace

Sarapeion

R H A K O T I S

Lake
Mareotis

Inner
Harbour

Heptastadion
Mole

Canal

Kibotos
Harbour

Eunostos
Harbour

Pharos   Island

NEKROPOLIS

MEDITERRANEAN
SEA

42

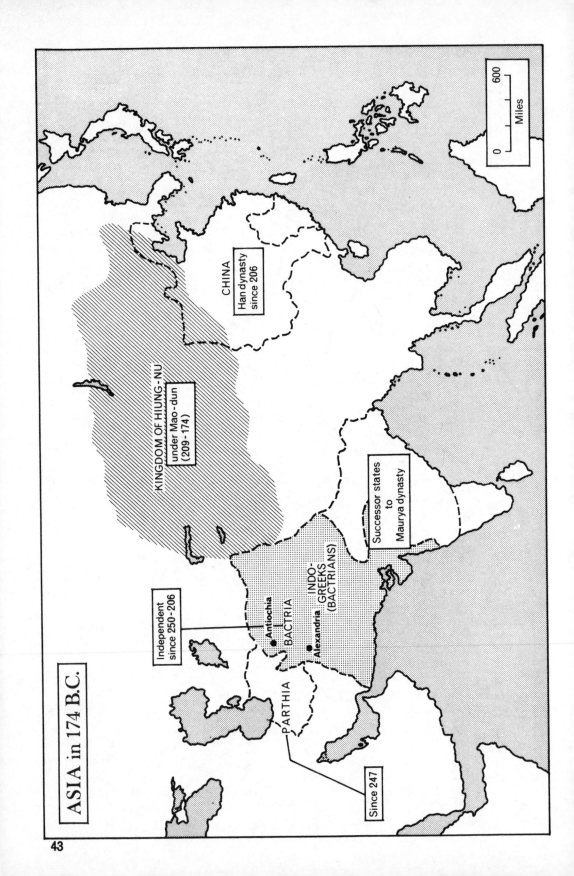

ASIA in 174 B.C.

600
Miles
0

KINGDOM OF HIUNG-NU
under Mao-dun
(209 - 174)

CHINA
Han dynasty
since 206

Successor states
to
Maurya dynasty

Independent
since 250 - 206

INDO-
GREEKS
(BACTRIANS)

Antiochia
BACTRIA

Alexandria

PARTHIA

Since 247

43

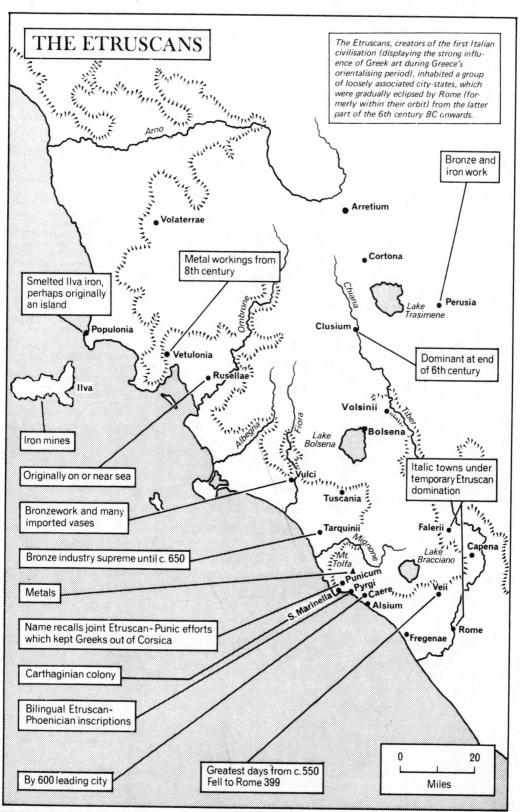

THE ETRUSCANS

The Etruscans, creators of the first Italian civilisation (displaying the strong influence of Greek art during Greece's orientalising period), inhabited a group of loosely associated city-states, which were gradually eclipsed by Rome (formerly within their orbit) from the latter part of the 6th century BC onwards.

Arno

Bronze and iron work

• Volaterrae

• Arretium

• Cortona

Metal workings from 8th century

Chiana

• Perusia

Lake Trasimene

Smelted Ilva iron, perhaps originally an island

Clusium

Dominant at end of 6th century

• Populonia

• Vetulonia

Ombrone

• Rusellae

Volsinii

Tiber

• Bolsena

Ilva

Albegna

Fiora

Lake Bolsena

Iron mines

Originally on or near sea

Vulci

Italic towns under temporary Etruscan domination

Bronzework and many imported vases

Tuscania

Falerii

Bronze industry supreme until c. 650

Tarquinii

Mignone

Capena

Lake Bracciano

Metals

Mt. Tolfa

Punicum

Pyrgi

Veii

Name recalls joint Etruscan-Punic efforts which kept Greeks out of Corsica

Caere

S. Marinella

Alsium

Rome

Carthaginian colony

Fregenae

Bilingual Etruscan-Phoenician inscriptions

By 600 leading city

Greatest days from c. 550 Fell to Rome 399

0   20

Miles

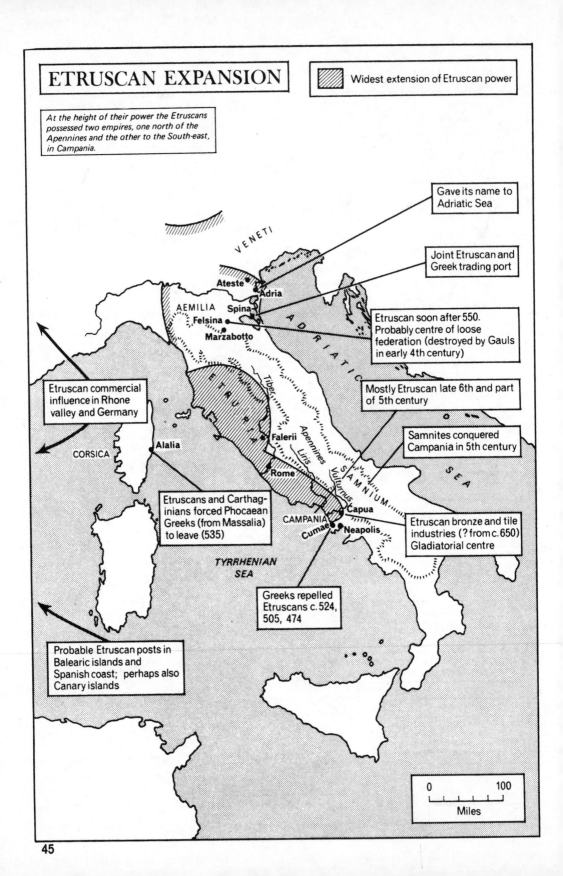

ETRUSCAN EXPANSION

▨ Widest extension of Etruscan power

At the height of their power the Etruscans possessed two empires, one north of the Apennines and the other to the South-east, in Campania.

Gave its name to Adriatic Sea

Joint Etruscan and Greek trading port

Etruscan soon after 550. Probably centre of loose federation (destroyed by Gauls in early 4th century)

Mostly Etruscan late 6th and part of 5th century

Samnites conquered Campania in 5th century

Etruscan commercial influence in Rhone valley and Germany

Etruscans and Carthaginians forced Phocaean Greeks (from Massalia) to leave (535)

Etruscan bronze and tile industries (? from c.650) Gladiatorial centre

Greeks repelled Etruscans c.524, 505, 474

Probable Etruscan posts in Balearic islands and Spanish coast; perhaps also Canary islands

VENETI

Ateste
Adria
AEMILIA   Spina
Felsina
Marzabotto

ADRIATIC

ETRURIA

Tiber

CORSICA
Alalia

Falerii
Apennines
Liris
Rome
Volturnus
SAMNIUM

SEA

CAMPANIA   Capua
Cumae   Neapolis

TYRRHENIAN SEA

0   100
Miles

45

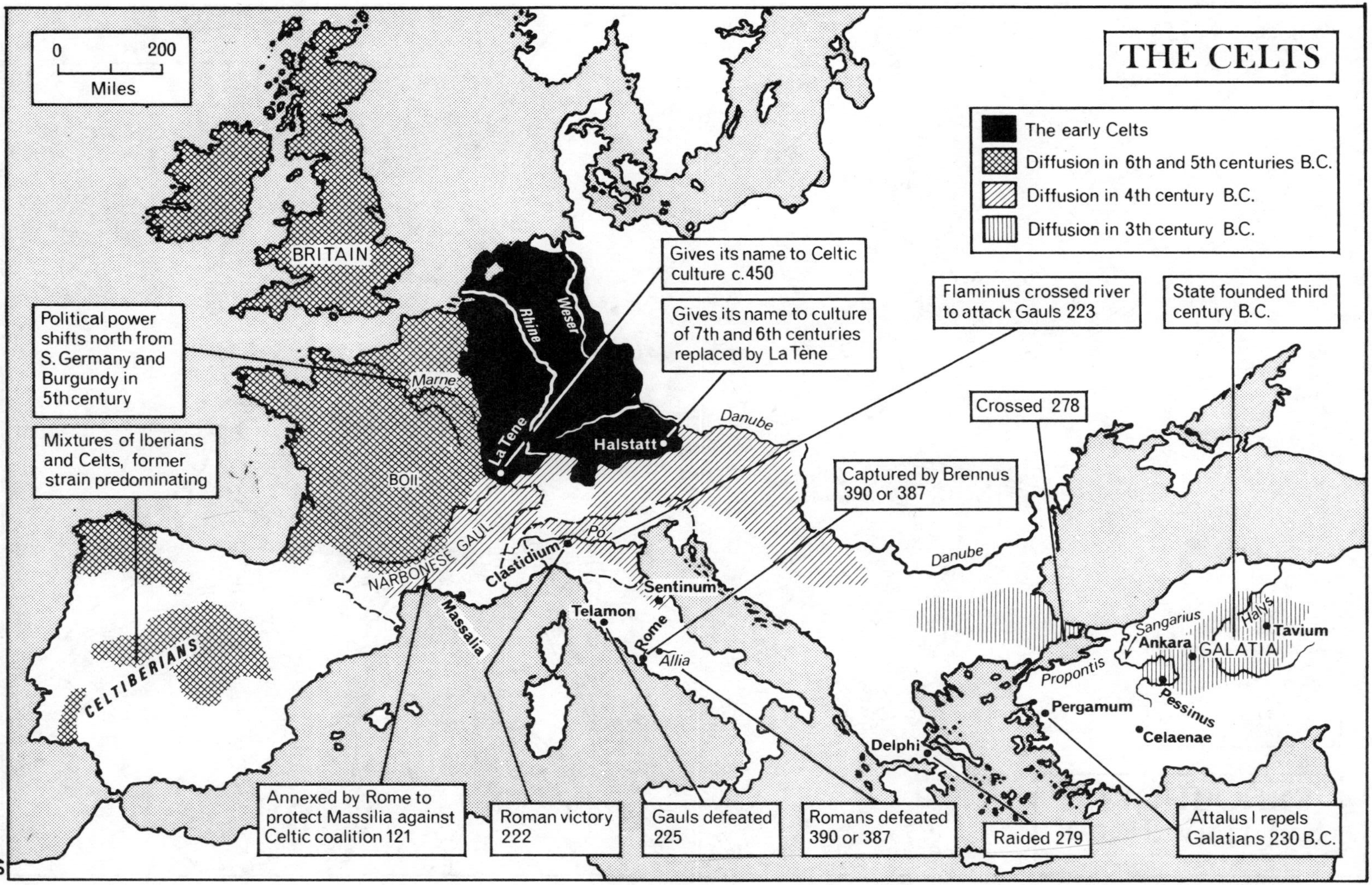
THE CELTS
The early Celts
Diffusion in 6th and 5th centuries B.C.
Diffusion in 4th century B.C.
Diffusion in 3th century B.C.
0
200
Miles
BRITAIN
BOII
NARBONESE GAUL
CELTIBERIANS
Marne
Rhine
Weser
La Tene
Halstatt
Danube
Po
Clastidium
Massalia
Telamon
Sentinum
Rome
Allia
Delphi
Propontis
Pergamum
Sangarius
Ankara
GALATIA
Halys
Tavium
Pessinus
Celaenae
Political power shifts north from S. Germany and Burgundy in 5th century
Mixtures of Iberians and Celts, former strain predominating
Gives its name to Celtic culture c.450
Gives its name to culture of 7th and 6th centuries replaced by La Tène
Flaminius crossed river to attack Gauls 223
State founded third century B.C.
Crossed 278
Captured by Brennus 390 or 387
Annexed by Rome to protect Massilia against Celtic coalition 121
Roman victory 222
Gauls defeated 225
Romans defeated 390 or 387
Raided 279
Attalus I repels Galatians 230 B.C.

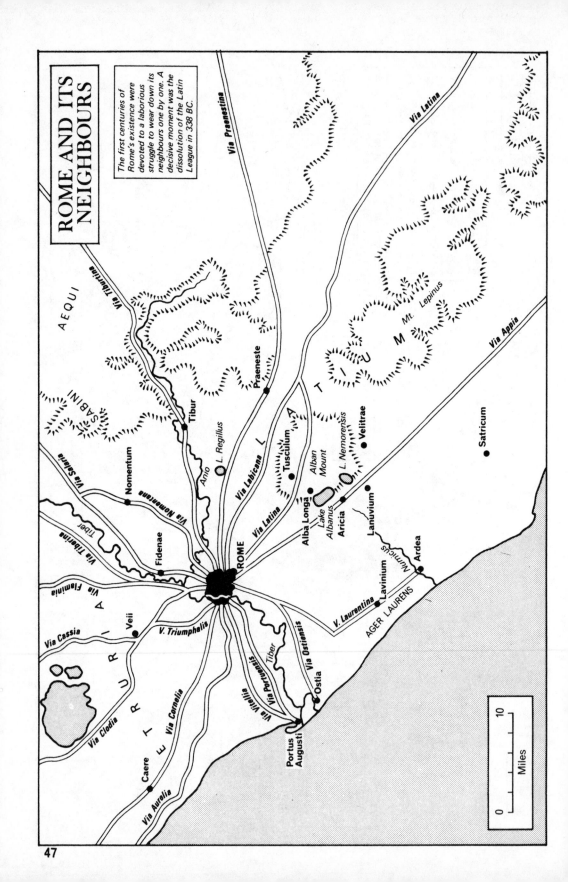

ROME AND ITS NEIGHBOURS

The first centuries of Rome's existence were devoted to a laborious struggle to wear down its neighbours one by one. A decisive moment was the dissolution of the Latin League in 338 BC.

Via Praenestina

Via Latina

Via Tiburtina

AEQUI

SABINI

Tibur

Nomentum

Via Salaria

Via Nomentana

Tiber

Anio

L. Regillus

Via Labicana

Via Latina

Praeneste

Mt. Lepinus

L A T I U M

Tusculum

Via Appis

Fidenae

Via Tiberina

Alba Longa

Lake Albanus

Alban Mount

Aricia

L. Nemorensis

Velitrae

Lanuvium

Satricum

Via Flaminia

ROME

Lavinium

Numicus

Ardea

Via Cassia

Veii

V. Triumphalis

E T R U R I A

Tiber

Via Ostiensis

V. Laurentina

AGER LAURENS

Via Vitellia

Via Portuensis

Via Cornelia

Ostia

Via Clodia

Portus Augusti

Caere

Via Aurelia

0   10

Miles

47

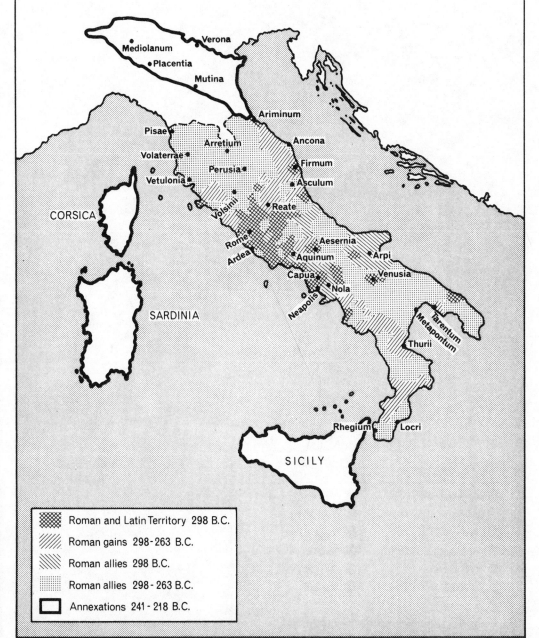

ROME'S CONQUEST OF ITALY

Third Samnite War 298-290
Invasion of Pyrrhus 280-275
First Punic War 264-241
Second Punic War 218-201
(see map 51)

0   100
Miles

Verona
Mediolanum
Placentia
Mutina
Ariminum
Pisae
Arretium
Ancona
Volaterrae
Perusia
Firmum
Vetulonia
Asculum
Volsinii
CORSICA
Reate
Rome
Aesernia
Ardea
Aquinum
Arpi
Capua
Venusia
Nola
Neapolis
SARDINIA
Tarentum
Metapontum
Thurii
Rhegium
Locri
SICILY

Roman and Latin Territory 298 B.C.
Roman gains 298-263 B.C.
Roman allies 298 B.C.
Roman allies 298-263 B.C.
Annexations 241-218 B.C.

THE ROADS OF ROMAN ITALY

0   100
Miles

CORSICA

SARDINIA

TYRRHENIAN SEA

SICILY

ADRIATIC SEA

Augusta Praetoria
Mediolanum
Segusio
Verona
Aquileia
Placentia
Cremona
Dertona
Mantua
Genua
Ravenna
Po
Ariminum
Luna
Florentia
Fanum Fortunae
Pisae
Vada Volaterrana
Arretium
Reate
Truentum
Tibur
Aternum
Corfinium
Anagnia
ROME
Fregellae
Tarracina
Cales
Casilinum
Capua
Beneventum
Canusium
Neapolis
Venusia
Brundisium
Tarentum
Rhegium

- **1** Via Aemilia (187 B.C.)
- **2** Via Appia (312 - 244 B.C.)
- **3** Via Aurelia
- **4** Via Flaminia (220 B.C.)
- **5** Via Latina
- **6** Via Postumia (148 B.C.)
- **7** Via Valeria
- **8** Via Julia Augusta
- **9** Via Domitiana
- **10** Via Trajana
- **11** Via Cassia
- **12** Via Popillia
- **13** Via Salaria

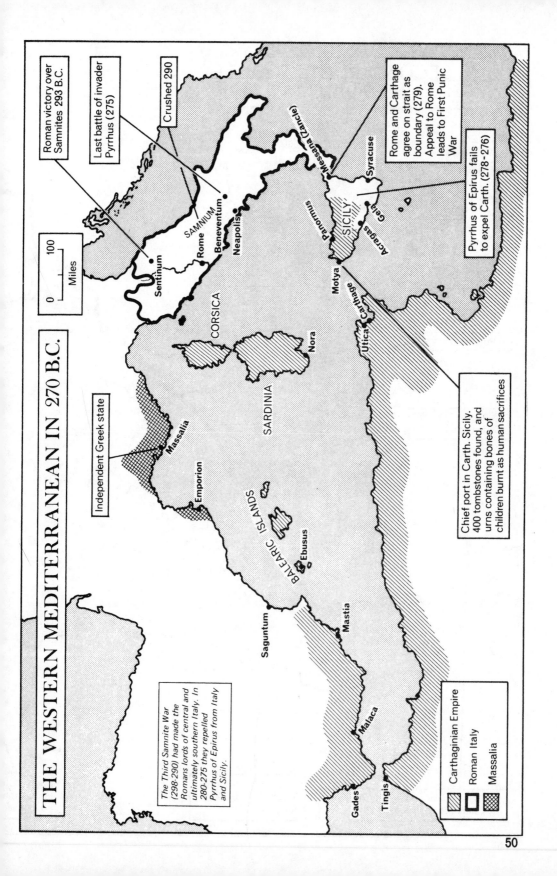

THE WESTERN MEDITERRANEAN IN 270 B.C.

Roman victory over Samnites 293 B.C.

Last battle of invader Pyrrhus (275)

Crushed 290

Rome and Carthage agree on strait as boundary (279). Appeal to Rome leads to First Punic War

Pyrrhus of Epirus fails to expel Carth. (278-276)

0   100
Miles

Independent Greek state

Chief port in Carth. Sicily. 400 tombstones found, and urns containing bones of children burnt as human sacrifices

The Third Samnite War (298-290) had made the Romans lords of central and ultimately southern Italy. In 280-275 they repelled Pyrrhus of Epirus from Italy and Sicily.

SAMNIUM
Rome
Sentium
Beneventum
Neapolis
Messana (Zancle)
Syracuse
Panormus
Gela
Acragas
SICILY
Motya
Utica
Carthage
CORSICA
SARDINIA
Nora
Massalia
Emporion
BALEARIC ISLANDS
Ebusus
Saguntum
Mastia
Malaca
Gades
Tingis

Carthaginian Empire
Roman Italy
Massalia

50

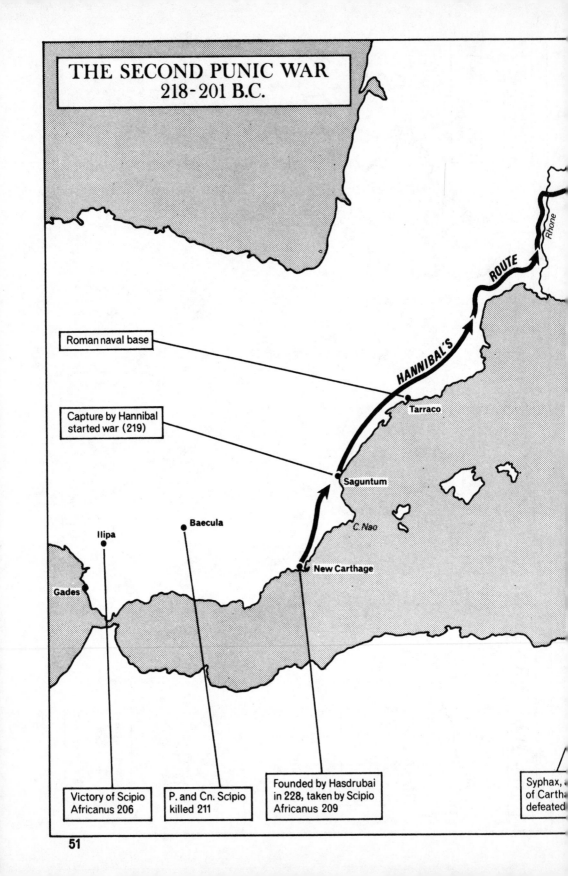

THE SECOND PUNIC WAR
218-201 B.C.

Rhone

HANNIBAL'S ROUTE

Roman naval base

Tarraco

Capture by Hannibal started war (219)

Saguntum

Baecula

C. Nao

Ilipa

New Carthage

Gades

Victory of Scipio Africanus 206

P. and Cn. Scipio killed 211

Founded by Hasdrubai in 228, taken by Scipio Africanus 209

Syphax, of Cartha defeated

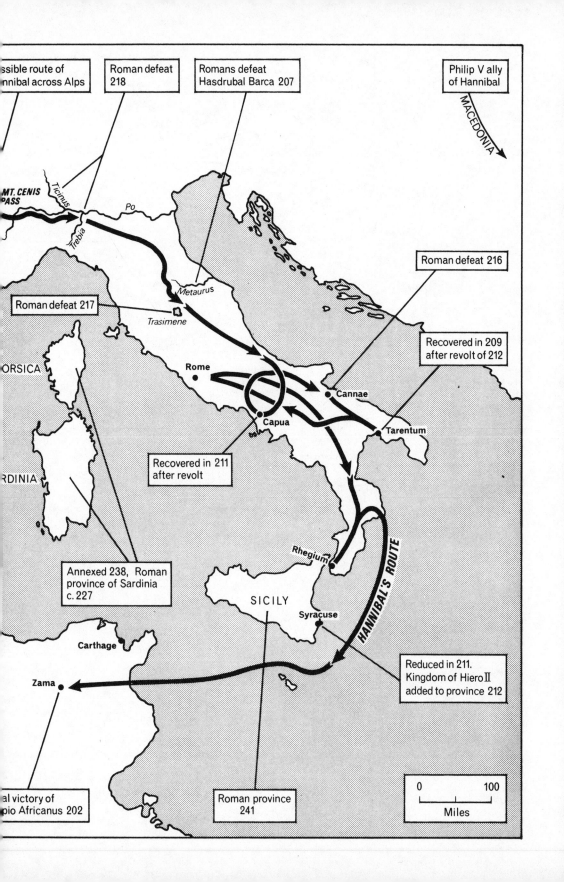

ssible route of
nnibal across Alps

Roman defeat
218

Romans defeat
Hasdrubal Barca 207

Philip V ally
of Hannibal

MACEDONIA

MT. CENIS
PASS

Ticinus

Po

Trebia

Roman defeat 216

Metaurus

Roman defeat 217

Trasimene

Recovered in 209
after revolt of 212

ORSICA

Rome

Cannae

RDINIA

Capua

Tarentum

Recovered in 211
after revolt

Annexed 238, Roman
province of Sardinia
c. 227

Rhegium

HANNIBAL'S ROUTE

SICILY

Syracuse

Carthage

Reduced in 211.
Kingdom of Hiero II
added to province 212

Zama

al victory of
pio Africanus 202

Roman province
241

0   100

Miles

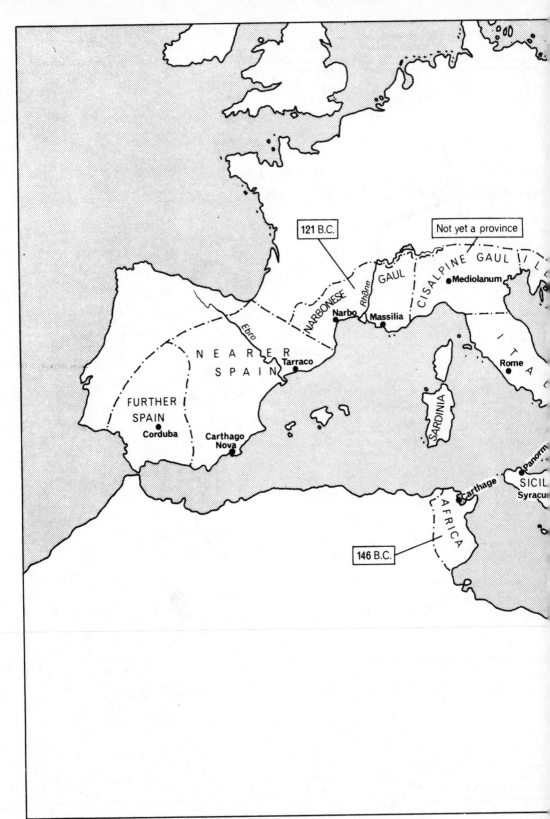

121 B.C.

Not yet a province

CISALPINE GAUL

Mediolanum

GAUL

Rhône

NARBONESE

Narbo

Massilia

Ebro

NEARER
SPAIN

Tarraco

Rome

FURTHER
SPAIN

SARDINIA

Corduba

Carthago
Nova

Panorm

SICIL

Carthage

Syracus

AFRICA

146 B.C.

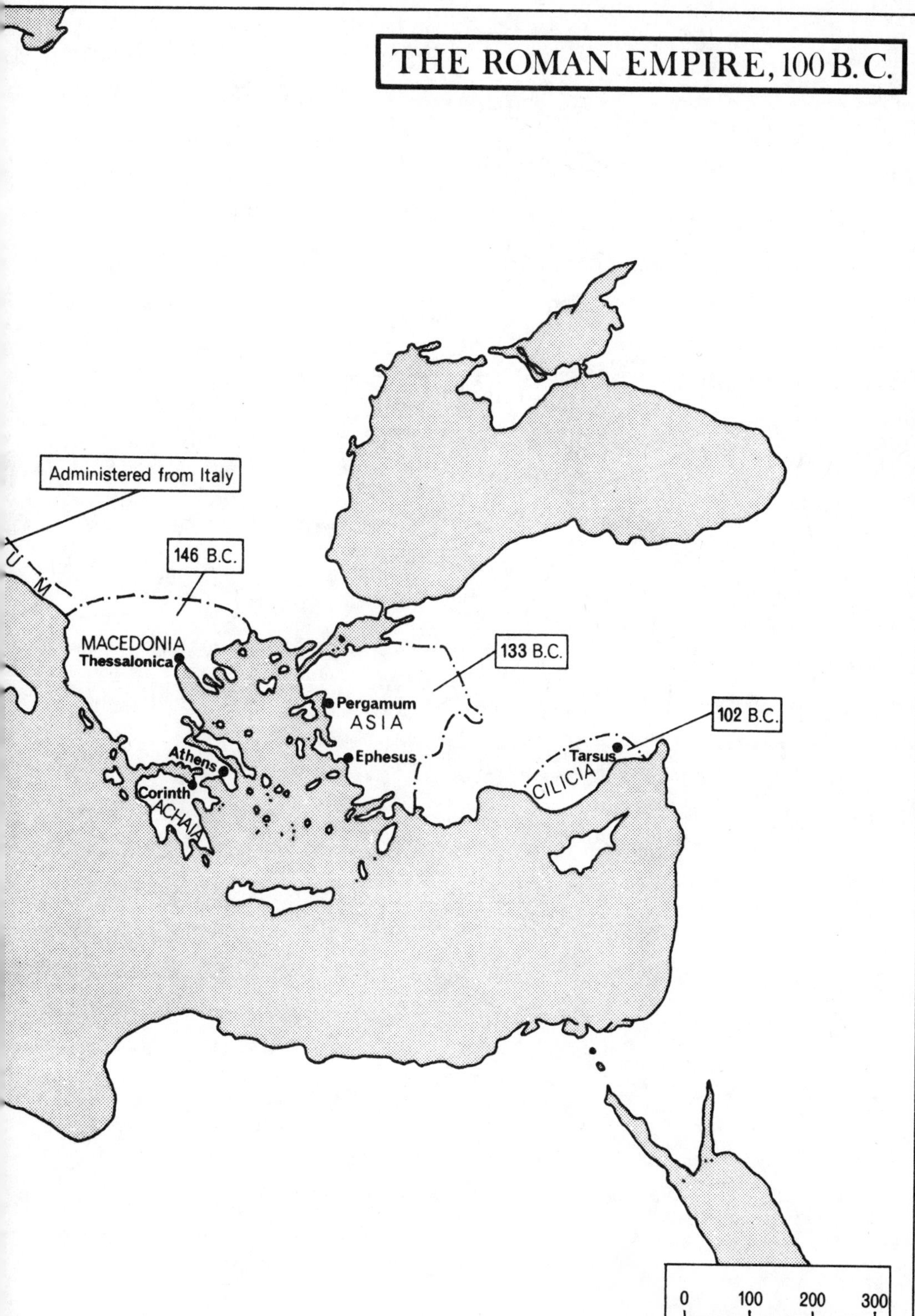

THE ROMAN EMPIRE, 100 B.C.

Administered from Italy

146 B.C.

133 B.C.

102 B.C.

MACEDONIA
Thessalonica

Pergamum
ASIA

Ephesus

Athens

Corinth

ACHAIA

Tarsus

CILICIA

0	100	200	300

Miles

BRITANNIA

GAUL
(GALLIA COMATA)

Conquered by
Caesar 58-51 B.C.

Citizenship granted
province 42 B.C.

Lugdunum

CISALPINE GAUL

Mediolanum

NARBONESE GAUL

Rhône

Narbo

Massilia

Rubicon

Rhine

Ebro

Ilerda

Tarraco

FURTHER
SPAIN

NEARER
SPAIN

ITALY

Rome

SARDINIA

Cordoba

Munda

Panormus

Carthage

Syracuse

SICILY

AFRICA

Cirta

AFRICA
NOVA

Province 46-30 B.C.

Thapsus

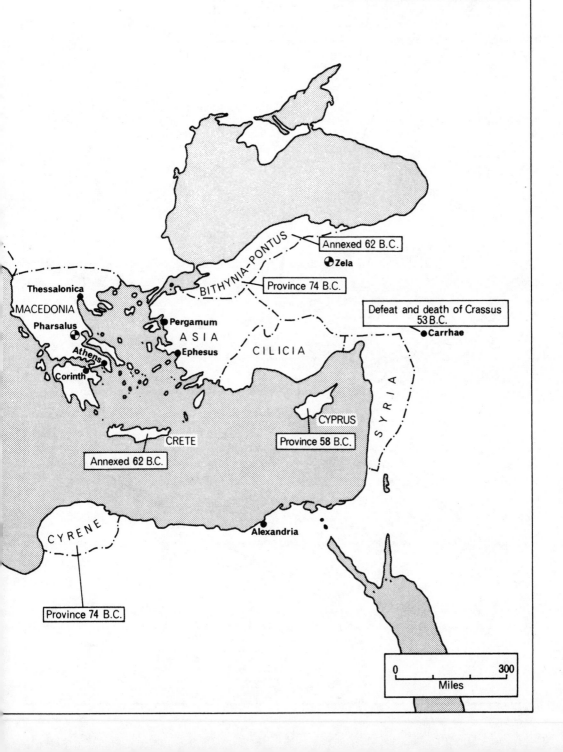

THE ROMAN EMPIRE, 44 B.C.

◑ Victories by Caesar in Civil War

Annexed 62 B.C.

◑ Zela

BITHYNIA-PONTUS

Province 74 B.C.

Defeat and death of Crassus
53 B.C.

● Carrhae

Thessalonica

MACEDONIA

Pergamum

Pharsalus

ASIA

Athens

Ephesus

CILICIA

Corinth

SYRIA

CYPRUS

CRETE

Province 58 B.C.

Annexed 62 B.C.

CYRENE

Alexandria

Province 74 B.C.

0   300

Miles

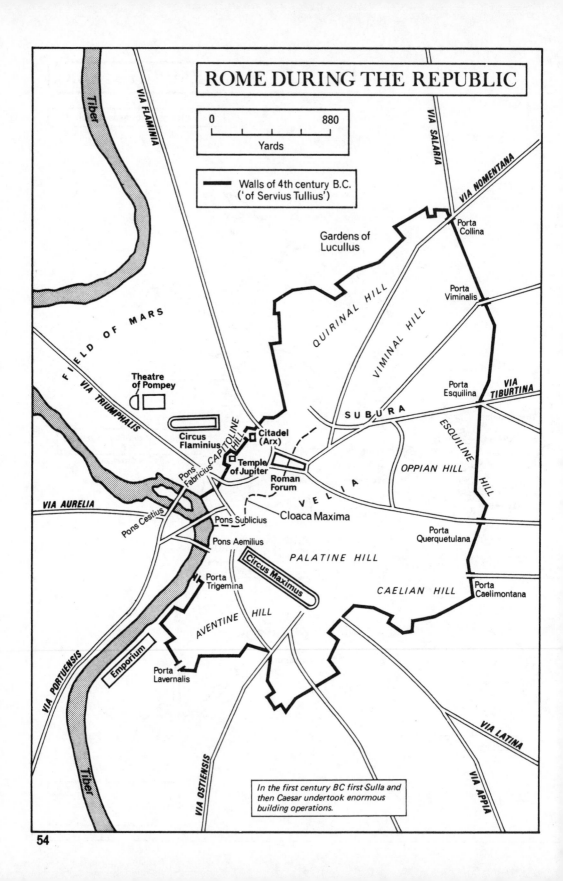

ROME DURING THE REPUBLIC

0 — 880

Yards

Walls of 4th century B.C.
('of Servius Tullius')

Tiber

VIA FLAMINIA

VIA SALARIA

VIA NOMENTANA

Porta
Collina

Gardens of
Lucullus

Porta
Viminalis

QUIRINAL HILL

VIMINAL HILL

F I E L D   O F   M A R S

VIA TRIUMPHALIS

Theatre
of Pompey

Porta
Esquilina

VIA
TIBURTINA

S U B U R A

ESQUILINE

Circus
Flaminius

CAPITOLINE HILL

Citadel
(Arx)

Temple
of Jupiter

Roman
Forum

V E L I A

OPPIAN HILL

HILL

Pons
Fabricius

VIA AURELIA

Pons Cestius

Pons Sublicius

Cloaca Maxima

Pons Aemilius

PALATINE HILL

Porta
Querquetulana

Circus Maximus

CAELIAN HILL

Porta
Caelimontana

Porta
Trigemina

AVENTINE   HILL

VIA PORTUENSIS

Emporium

Porta
Lavernalis

Tiber

VIA OSTIENSIS

VIA APPIA

VIA LATINA

*In the first century BC first Sulla and
then Caesar undertook enormous
building operations.*

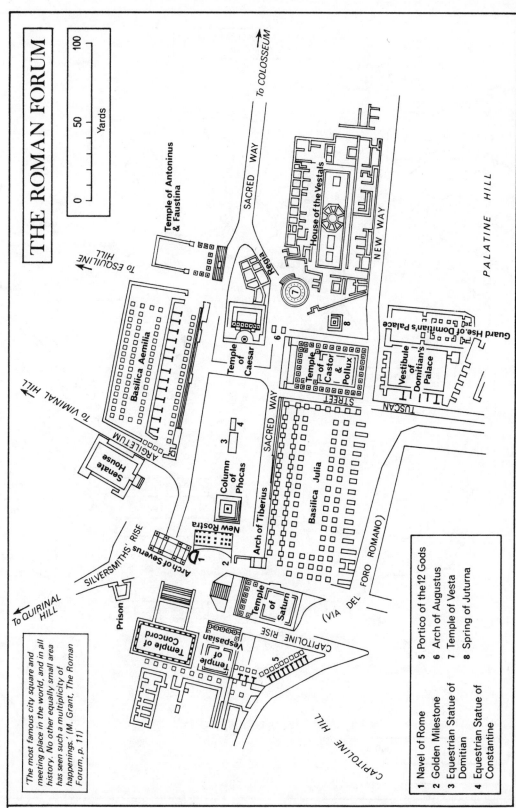

THE ROMAN FORUM

0 50 100

Yards

'The most famous city square and meeting place in the world, and in all history. No other equally small area has seen such a multiplicity of happenings.' (M. Grant, The Roman Forum, p. 11)

To COLOSSEUM

SACRED WAY

Temple of Antoninus & Faustina

To ESQUILINE HILL

Regia

House of the Vestals

NEW WAY

PALATINE HILL

Basilica Aemilia

To VIMINAL HILL

Temple of Caesar

ARGILETUM

Senate House

Column of Phocas

3

4

Temple of Castor & Pollux

STREET

6

8

Guard Hse. of Domitian's Palace

Vestibule of Domitian's Palace

TUSCAN

SACRED WAY

Basilica Julia

SILVERSMITHS' RISE

Arch of Tiberius

New Rostra

1

Arch of Severus

2

To QUIRINAL HILL

Prison

Temple of Concord

Temple of Saturn

Temple of Vespasian

CAPITOLINE RISE

5

(VIA DEL FORO ROMANO)

CAPITOLINE HILL

1 Navel of Rome
2 Golden Milestone
3 Equestrian Statue of Domitian
4 Equestrian Statue of Constantine
5 Portico of the 12 Gods
6 Arch of Augustus
7 Temple of Vesta
8 Spring of Juturna

55

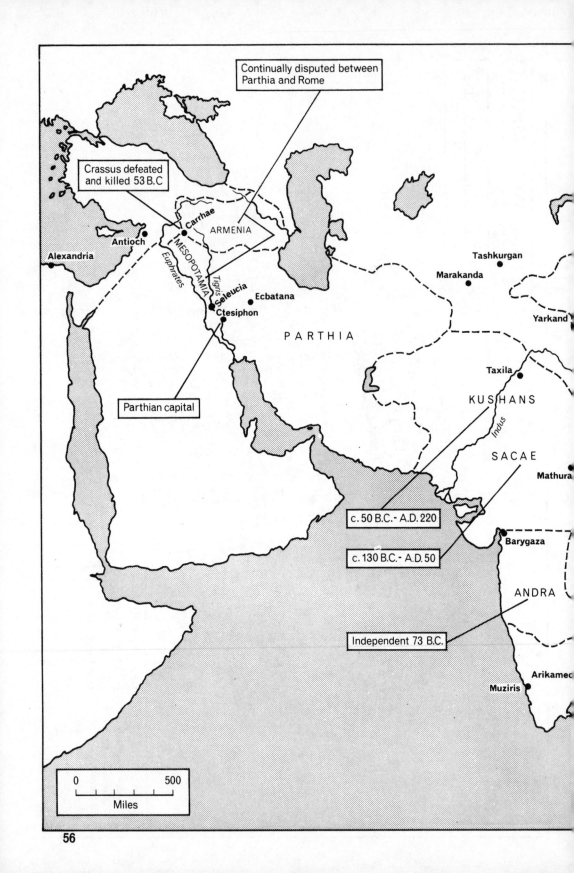

Continually disputed between
Parthia and Rome

Crassus defeated
and killed 53 B.C

Tashkurgan

Marakanda

Carrhae
ARMENIA

Antioch

Alexandria

Yarkand

MESOPOTAMIA

Euphrates

Tigris

Seleucia

Ecbatana

Ctesiphon

P A R T H I A

Taxila

KUSHANS

Parthian capital

Indus

S A C A E

Mathura

c. 50 B.C.- A.D. 220

c. 130 B.C.- A.D. 50

Barygaza

ANDRA

Independent 73 B.C.

Arikamed

Muziris

0   500
Miles

PARTHIA AND THE EAST

Chinese c 100 B.C.- 9 A.D. and from 60 A.D.

Capital of Earlier (Western) Han 202 B.C.

Capital of Later (Eastern) Han A.D. 23

IUNG-NU

SHGARIA

Hwang-ho

Loyang

Ch'ang-an (Sian)

Yangtse

CHINA

Pataliputra (Patna)

Ganges

MAGHADA

NGA

Palura

Independent 157 B.C.

The Parthian Empire, the only major power on Rome's frontiers, was a loose feudal structure created by the Arsacid dynasty in c 248-7 BC. It was overthrown by the Sassanian Persians in AD 223-6. The capital of both empires was Ctesiphon, across the Tigris from the Greek city of **Seleucia**

BRITANNIA

FREE GERMANY

LWR. GERMANY (17 B.C.)

Temporarily conquered from 15 B.C. but abandoned after ambushing of Varus by Arminius in A.D.9

Colonia Agrippinensis

Rhine

B E L G I C A

Moguntiacum

Danube

LOWER PANNONIA (1 B

LUGDUNENSIS

UPR. GERMANY (17 B.C.)

RHAETIA (15 B.C.)

NORICUM (15 B.C.)

UPPER PANNONIA

Lugdunum

P

Aquileia

AQUITANIA

C

M

NARBONENSIS

Nemausus

I T A L Y

Adriatic Sea

Rome

TARRACONENSIS

Tarraco

Corsica

LUSITANIA (c. 27 B.C.)

Corduba

BAETICA

Naulochus

SICILY

Gades

Carthage

M A U R E T A N I A

Naval victory ov Sextus Pompei 36 B.C.

A F R I C A

Imperial frontier as in A.D.14

Provincial frontiers

ASIA Senatorial provinces

ALPINE PROVINCES (15-14 B.C.)
M: Maritime, C: Cottian, P: Pennine

The hatched areas represent the more important dependent ('client') states, whose monarchs enjoyed internal autonomy but had to support Rome's foreign policy and help defend the imperial frontiers.

/////// Principal client states

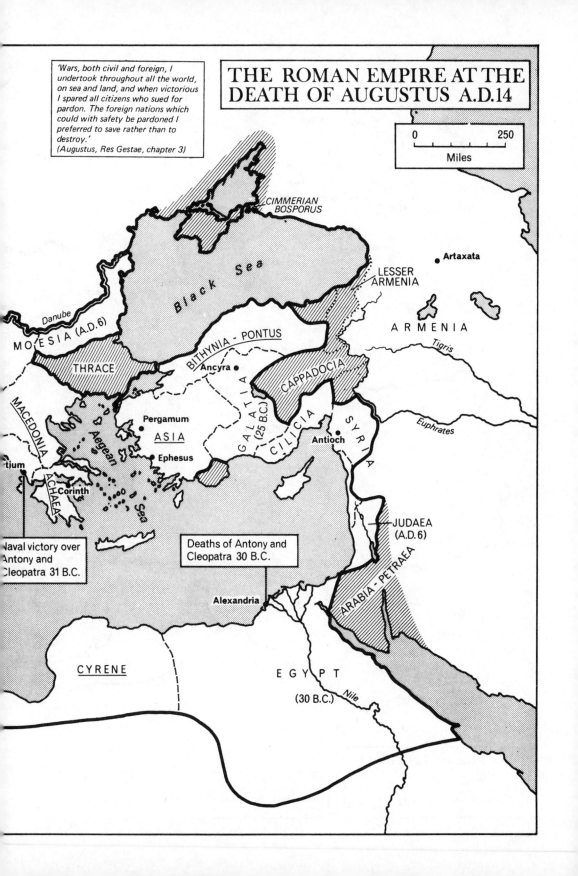

'Wars, both civil and foreign, I
undertook throughout all the world,
on sea and land, and when victorious
I spared all citizens who sued for
pardon. The foreign nations which
could with safety be pardoned I
preferred to save rather than to
destroy.'
(Augustus, Res Gestae, chapter 3)

THE ROMAN EMPIRE AT THE
DEATH OF AUGUSTUS A.D.14

0   250
Miles

CIMMERIAN
BOSPORUS

• Artaxata

Black Sea

LESSER
ARMENIA

Danube

A R M E N I A

MOESIA (A.D.6)

BITHYNIA - PONTUS

Tigris

THRACE

Ancyra •

CAPPADOCIA

MACEDONIA

GALATIA
(25 B.C.)

CILICIA

SYRIA

Euphrates

Pergamum

ASIA

Antioch •

Aegean

Ephesus

tium

ACHAEA

Corinth

JUDAEA
(A.D.6)

Naval victory over
Antony and
Cleopatra 31 B.C.

Deaths of Antony and
Cleopatra 30 B.C.

ARABIA - PETRAEA

Alexandria

CYRENE

E G Y P T

(30 B.C.)

Nile

GAUL

SPAIN

Ebro

Rhine

Danube

Adriatic Sea

Rhone

Arelate

VIA DOMITIA

Narbo

Forum Julii

I·T·A

Rome

Tyrrhenian Sea

Mediterranean

AFRICA

All roads lead to Rome: the most potent guarantees of external and internal peace and stimulants of prosperity.

Imperial frontier as in A.D. 14
Roman roads
Mountain contours

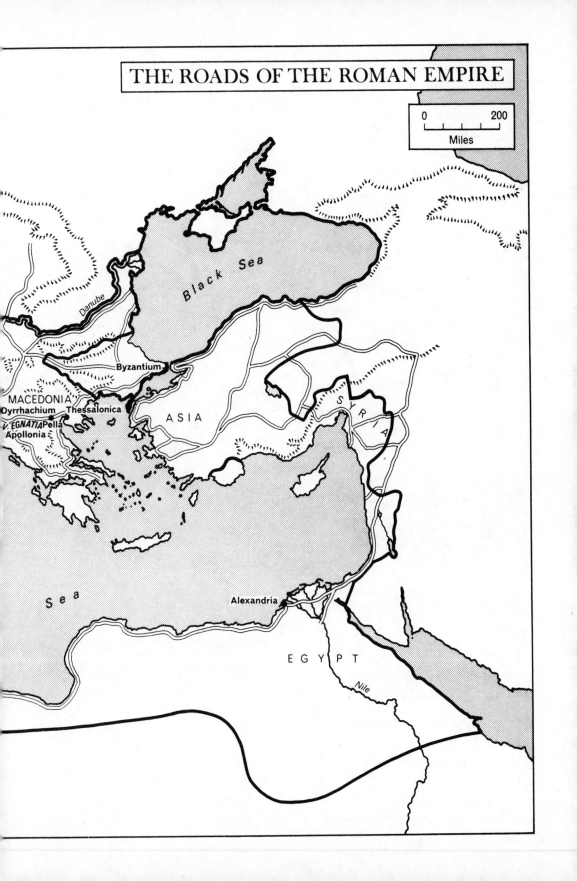

THE ROADS OF THE ROMAN EMPIRE

0   200

Miles

Black Sea

Danube

Byzantium

MACEDONIA
Dyrrhachium   Thessalonica
V EGNATIA Pella
Apollonia

ASIA

SYRIA

Sea

Alexandria

EGYPT

Nile

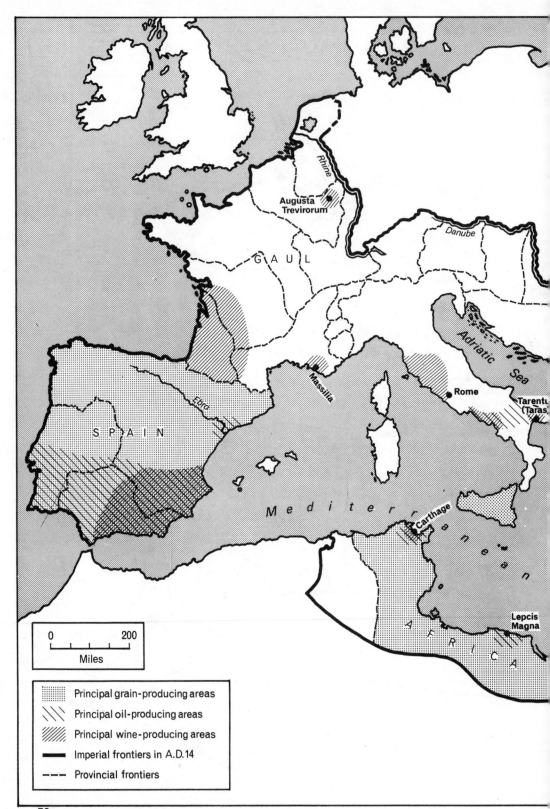

Augusta
Trevirorum

Rhine

Danube

GAUL

Adriatic Sea

Massilia

Rome

Tarentum
(Taras)

Ebro

SPAIN

Mediterranean

Carthage

AFRICA

Lepcis
Magna

0	200

Miles

Principal grain-producing areas

Principal oil-producing areas

Principal wine-producing areas

Imperial frontiers in A.D.14

Provincial frontiers

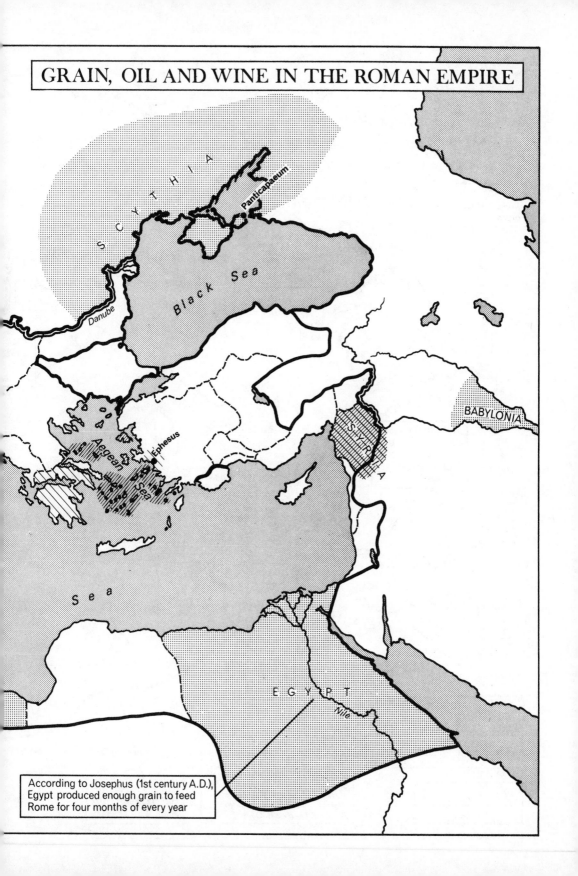

GRAIN, OIL AND WINE IN THE ROMAN EMPIRE

S C Y T H I A

Panticapaeum

Black Sea

Danube

BABYLONIA

Aegean

Ephesus

S Y R I A

Sea

Sea

EGYPT

Nile

According to Josephus (1st century A.D.),
Egypt produced enough grain to feed
Rome for four months of every year

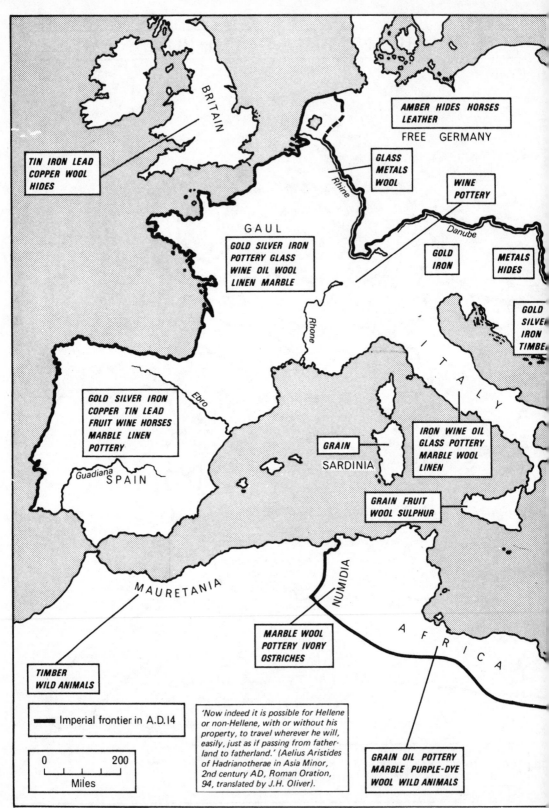

BRITAIN

TIN IRON LEAD
COPPER WOOL
HIDES

AMBER HIDES HORSES
LEATHER

FREE GERMANY

GLASS
METALS
WOOL

WINE
POTTERY

Rhine

Danube

GAUL

GOLD SILVER IRON
POTTERY GLASS
WINE OIL WOOL
LINEN MARBLE

GOLD
IRON

METALS
HIDES

GOLD
SILVER
IRON
TIMBER

Rhone

I T A L Y

Ebro

GOLD SILVER IRON
COPPER TIN LEAD
FRUIT WINE HORSES
MARBLE LINEN
POTTERY

GRAIN

SARDINIA

IRON WINE OIL
GLASS POTTERY
MARBLE WOOL
LINEN

Guadiana SPAIN

GRAIN FRUIT
WOOL SULPHUR

MAURETANIA

NUMIDIA

A F R I C A

MARBLE WOOL
POTTERY IVORY
OSTRICHES

TIMBER
WILD ANIMALS

——— Imperial frontier in A.D.14

0   200

Miles

'Now indeed it is possible for Hellene
or non-Hellene, with or without his
property, to travel wherever he will,
easily, just as if passing from fatherland to fatherland.' (Aelius Aristides
of Hadrianotherae in Asia Minor,
2nd century AD, Roman Oration,
94, translated by J.H. Oliver).

GRAIN OIL POTTERY
MARBLE PURPLE-DYE
WOOL WILD ANIMALS

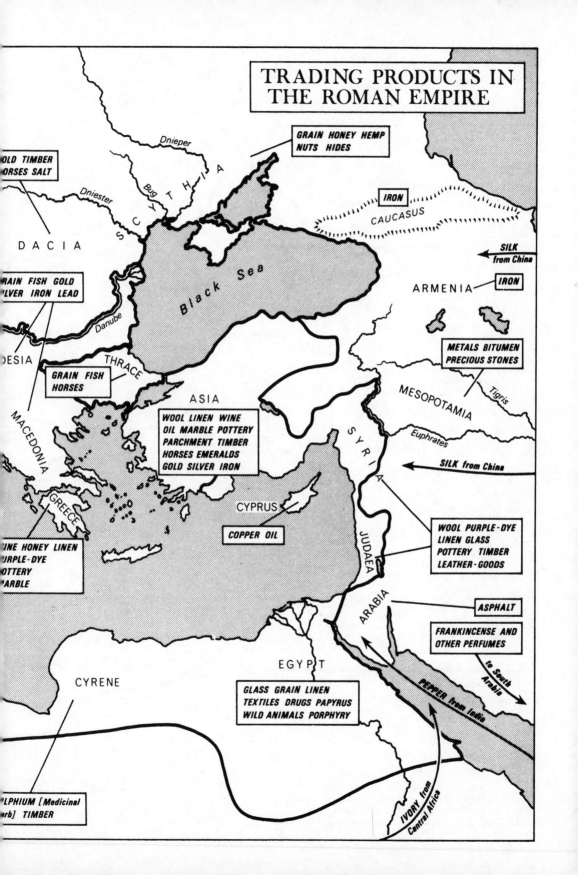

TRADING PRODUCTS IN THE ROMAN EMPIRE

Dnieper

GRAIN HONEY HEMP
NUTS HIDES

GOLD TIMBER
HORSES SALT

Dniester

Bug

S C Y T H I A

IRON

CAUCASUS

D A C I A

SILK
from China

ARMENIA

IRON

GRAIN FISH GOLD
SILVER IRON LEAD

Black Sea

Danube

METALS BITUMEN
PRECIOUS STONES

MOESIA

THRACE

GRAIN FISH
HORSES

MESOPOTAMIA

Tigris

MACEDONIA

ASIA

WOOL LINEN WINE
OIL MARBLE POTTERY
PARCHMENT TIMBER
HORSES EMERALDS
GOLD SILVER IRON

S
Y
R
I
A

Euphrates

SILK from China

GREECE

CYPRUS

COPPER OIL

WOOL PURPLE-DYE
LINEN GLASS
POTTERY TIMBER
LEATHER-GOODS

WINE HONEY LINEN
PURPLE-DYE
POTTERY
MARBLE

J
U
D
A
E
A

A
R
A
B
I
A

ASPHALT

FRANKINCENSE AND
OTHER PERFUMES

to South
Arabia

CYRENE

EGYPT

GLASS GRAIN LINEN
TEXTILES DRUGS PAPYRUS
WILD ANIMALS PORPHYRY

PEPPER from India

SILPHIUM [Medicinal
Herb] TIMBER

IVORY from
Central Africa

Major mints. Date at which Rome supersedes Lugdunum uncertain. Designs of copper, and perhaps for a time silver coins, imitated at many other mints.

BELGICA

LUGDUNENSIS

GAUL

RHAETIA

NORICUM

Extensive bronze city-coinages cease under Caligula (A.D. 37 - 41)

AQUITANIA

Lugdunum ◆□■▲

NARBONENSIS

Nemausus ●○

ILLYRICUM

I T A L Y

Rome ■▲□◆

TARRACONENSIS

SPAIN ○

Large temporary city-coinage circulates through-out west

LUSITANIA

BAETICA

NUMIDIA

AFRICA ○

■ Gold

▲ Silver

△ Base silver

□ Brass

○ Bronze

◆ Copper

Note: Augustus reformed and enlarged the Roman imperial coinage, issuing gold, silver, brass and copper on an enormous scale

Small bronze city-coinage virtually cease under Tiberius (A.D. 14)

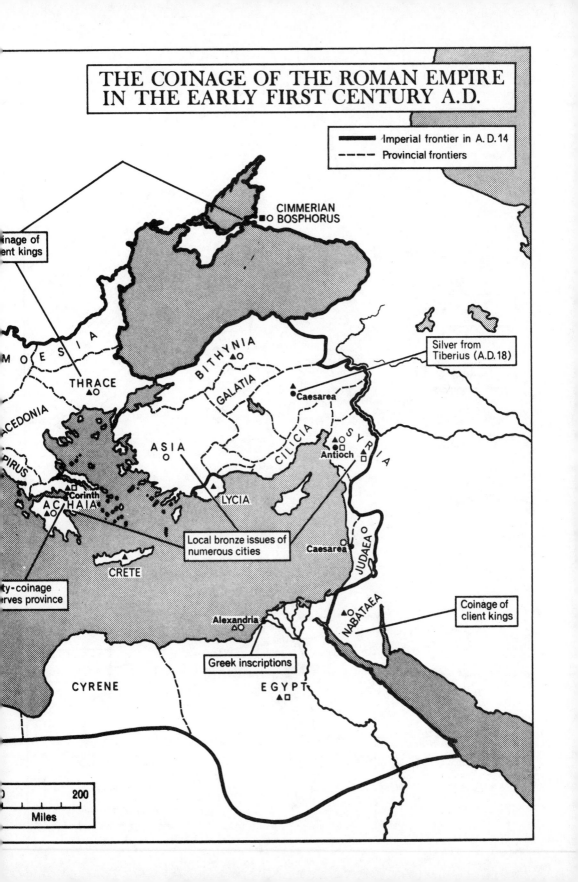

THE COINAGE OF THE ROMAN EMPIRE IN THE EARLY FIRST CENTURY A.D.

Imperial frontier in A.D. 14
Provincial frontiers

CIMMERIAN BOSPHORUS

...inage of ...ent kings

Silver from Tiberius (A.D. 18)

MOESIA

THRACE

BITHYNIA

GALATIA

Caesarea

MACEDONIA

EPIRUS

ASIA

CILICIA

SYRIA

Antioch

Corinth

ACHAIA

LYCIA

Local bronze issues of numerous cities

Caesarea

JUDAEA

CRETE

...ty-coinage ...rves province

NABATAEA

Coinage of client kings

Alexandria

Greek inscriptions

CYRENE

EGYPT

200

Miles

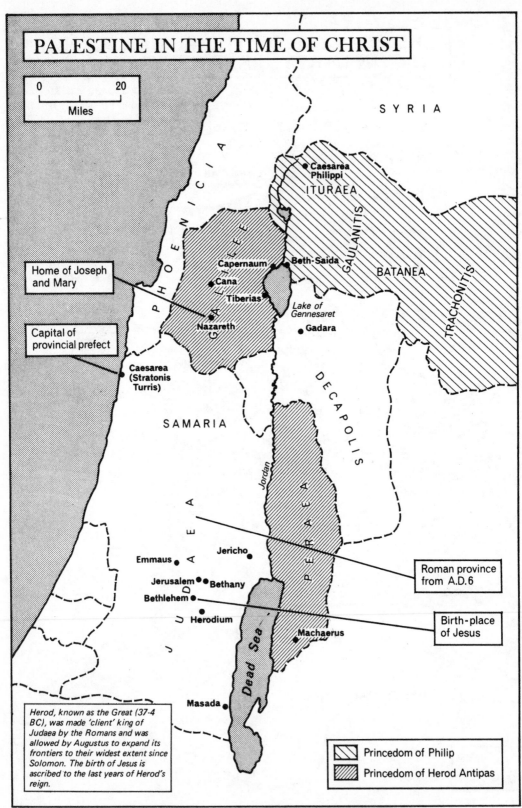

PALESTINE IN THE TIME OF CHRIST

0   20
Miles

SYRIA

Caesarea
Philippi

ITURAEA

GAULANITIS

BATANEA

TRACHONITIS

PHOENICIA

GALILEE

Capernaum
Cana
Beth-Saida
Tiberias

Lake of
Gennesaret

Nazareth

Gadara

Home of Joseph
and Mary

Capital of
provincial prefect

Caesarea
(Stratonis
Turris)

DECAPOLIS

SAMARIA

Jordan

PERAEA

JUDAEA

Jericho

Emmaus

Jerusalem Bethany
Bethlehem

Herodium

Dead Sea

Machaerus

Roman province
from A.D. 6

Birth-place
of Jesus

Masada

*Herod, known as the Great (37-4
BC), was made 'client' king of
Judaea by the Romans and was
allowed by Augustus to expand its
frontiers to their widest extent since
Solomon. The birth of Jesus is
ascribed to the last years of Herod's
reign.*

Princedom of Philip

Princedom of Herod Antipas

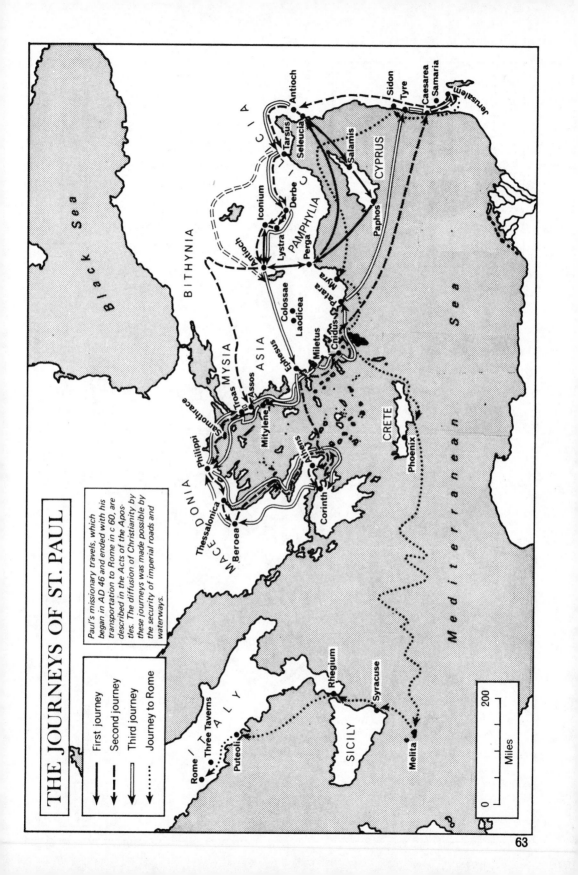

THE JOURNEYS OF ST. PAUL

Paul's missionary travels, which began in AD 46 and ended with his transportation to Rome in c 60, are described in the Acts of the Apostles. The diffusion of Christianity by these journeys was made possible by the security of imperial roads and waterways.

First journey
Second journey
Third journey
Journey to Rome

Black Sea

BITHYNIA

CILICIA

Tarsus
Seleucia
Antioch
Salamis
CYPRUS
Paphos
Perga
PAMPHYLIA
Antioch
Lystra
Derbe
Iconium

Sidon
Tyre
Caesarea
Samaria
Jerusalem

Myra
Patara
Cnidus
Colossae
Laodicea
Miletus
Ephesus
ASIA
MYSIA
Assos
Troas
Samothrace
Mitylene

Mediterranean Sea

CRETE
Phoenix

MACEDONIA
Philippi
Thessalonica
Beroea
Athens
Corinth

ITALY
Rome
Three Taverns
Puteoli
Rhegium
Syracuse
SICILY
Melita

0   200
Miles

63

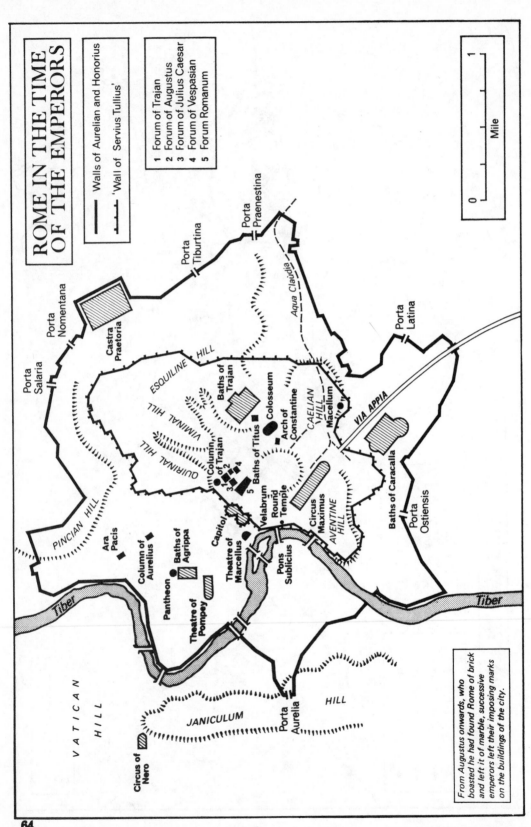

ROME IN THE TIME OF THE EMPERORS

—— Walls of Aurelian and Honorius

—·—·— 'Wall of Servius Tullius'

1 Forum of Trajan
2 Forum of Augustus
3 Forum of Julius Caesar
4 Forum of Vespasian
5 Forum Romanum

0   1

Mile

Porta Nomentana

Porta Salaria

Castra Praetoria

Porta Tiburtina

Porta Praenestina

Aqua Claudia

ESQUILINE HILL

VIMINAL HILL

QUIRINAL HILL

Baths of Trajan

Colosseum

Arch of Constantine

CAELIAN HILL

Macellum

Porta Latina

VIA APPIA

Column of Trajan

Baths of Titus

1
2
3 4
5

Velabrum
Round Temple

Circus Maximus

AVENTINE HILL

Baths of Caracalla

Porta Ostiensis

PINCIAN HILL

Ara Pacis

Column of Aurelius

Pantheon

Baths of Agrippa

Theatre of Pompey

Capitol

Theatre of Marcellus

Pons Sublicius

Tiber

Tiber

VATICAN HILL

JANICULUM HILL

Porta Aurelia

Circus of Nero

From Augustus onwards, who boasted he had found Rome of brick and left it of marble, successive emperors left their imposing marks on the buildings of the city.

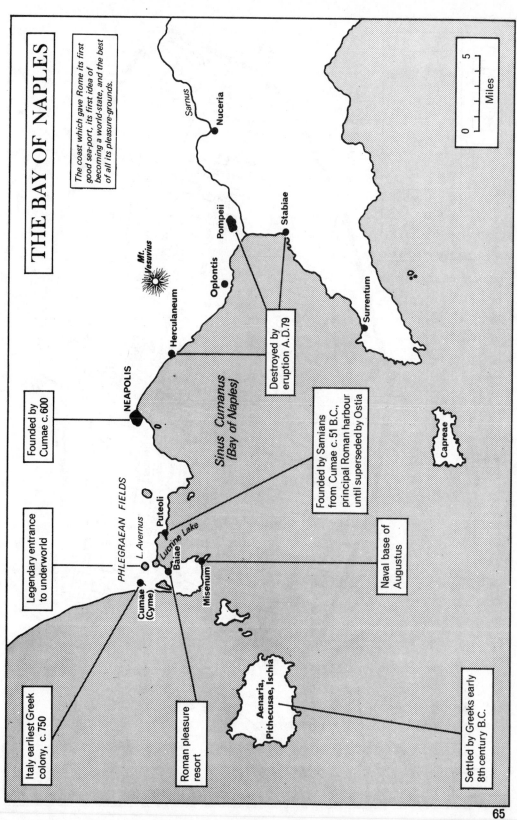

THE BAY OF NAPLES

The coast which gave Rome its first good sea-port, its first idea of becoming a world-state, and the best of all its pleasure-grounds.

Sarnus

Nuceria

Mt. Vesuvius

Oplontis

Pompeii

Herculaneum

Stabiae

Surrentum

NEAPOLIS

Founded by Cumae c. 600

Sinus Cumanus (Bay of Naples)

Destroyed by eruption A.D. 79

PHLEGRAEAN FIELDS

Puteoli

L. Avernus

Lucrine Lake

Baiae

Legendary entrance to underworld

Cumae (Cyme)

Misenum

Founded by Samians from Cumae c. 51 B.C., principal Roman harbour until superseded by Ostia

Naval base of Augustus

Capreae

Italy earliest Greek colony, c. 750

Roman pleasure resort

Aenaria, Pithecusae, Ischia

Settled by Greeks early 8th century B.C.

0 5
Miles

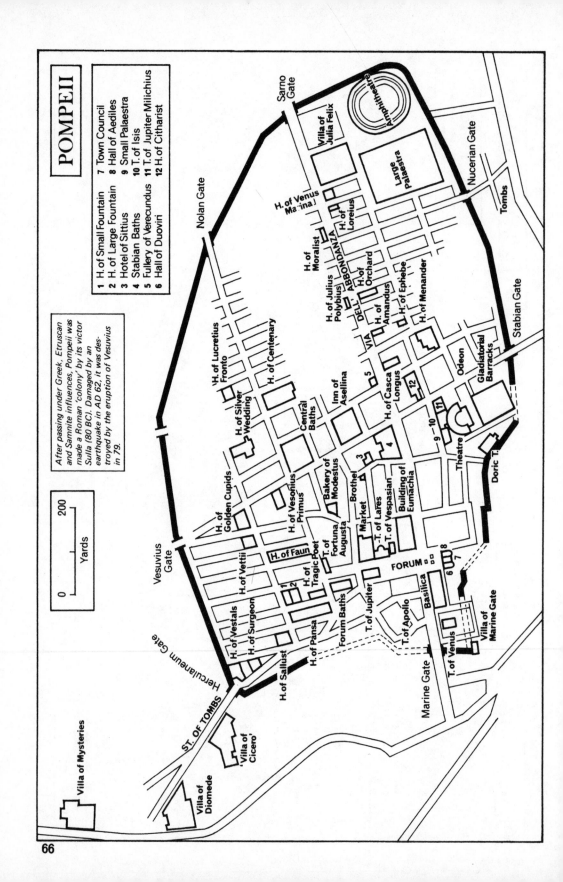

POMPEII

1 H. of Small Fountain
2 H. of Large Fountain
3 Hotel of Sittius
4 Stabian Baths
5 Fullery of Verecundus
6 Hall of Duoviri
7 Town Council
8 Hall of Aediles
9 Small Palaestra
10 T. of Isis
11 T. of Jupiter Milichius
12 H. of Citharist

After passing under Greek, Etruscan and Samnite influences, Pompeii was made a Roman 'colony' by its victor Sulla (80 BC). Damaged by an earthquake in AD 62, it was destroyed by the eruption of Vesuvius in 79.

0   200
Yards

Sarno Gate
Nucerian Gate
Tombs
Stabian Gate

Villa of Julia Felix
Amphitheatre
Large Palaestra

H. of Venus Marina
H. of Loreius
DELL' ABBONDANZA
VIA
H. of Orchard
H. of Amandus
H. of Ephebe
H. of Menander
H. of Moralist
H. of Julius Polybius

Nolan Gate

H. of Lucretius Fronto
H. of Centenary
H. of Silver Wedding
Central Baths
Inn of Asellina
H. of Casca Longus
5
12
Odeon
Gladiatorial Barracks
9 – 10
11
Theatre
Doric T.

H. of Golden Cupids
H. of Vesonius Primus
Bakery of Modestus
3
4
Brothel
Market
T. of Lares
T. of Vespasian
Building of Eumachia
FORUM
8
7
6

Vesuvius Gate

H. of Faun
T. of Tragic Poet
T. of Fortuna Augusta
T. of Jupiter
Basilica
T. of Apollo

H. of Vettii
H. of Pansa
Forum Baths
T. of Venus
Villa of Venus

H. of Vestals
H. of Surgeon
H. of Sallust

Herculaneum Gate
ST. OF TOMBS

Marine Gate
Villa of Marine Gate

'Villa of Cicero'
Villa of Diomede
Villa of Mysteries

66

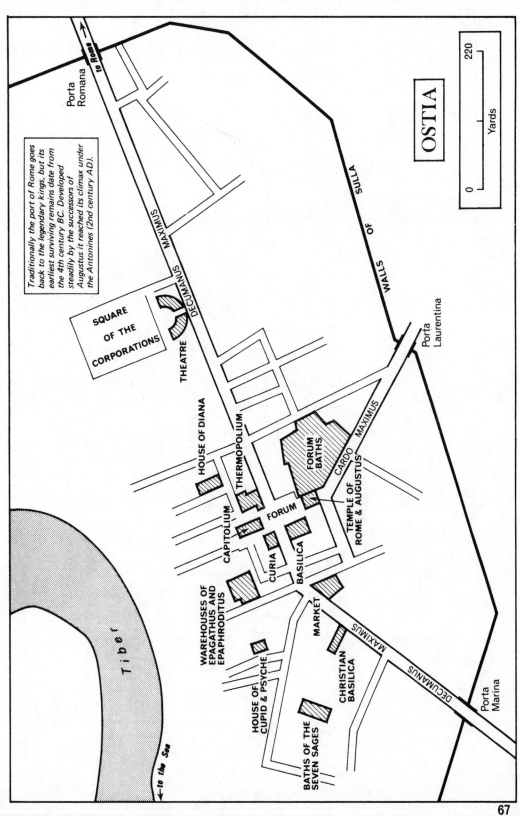

OSTIA

Yards
0   220

Traditionally the port of Rome goes back to the legendary kings, but its earliest surviving remains date from the 4th century BC. Developed steadily by the successors of Augustus it reached its climax under the Antonines (2nd century AD).

to Rome

Porta Romana

DECUMANUS MAXIMUS

SQUARE OF THE CORPORATIONS

THEATRE

HOUSE OF DIANA

THERMOPOLIUM

CAPITOLIUM

FORUM BATHS

CARDO MAXIMUS

CURIA

FORUM

BASILICA

TEMPLE OF ROME & AUGUSTUS

WALLS OF SULLA

Porta Laurentina

WAREHOUSES OF EPAGATHUS AND EPAPHRODITUS

MARKET

HOUSE OF CUPID & PSYCHE

DECUMANUS MAXIMUS

CHRISTIAN BASILICA

Porta Marina

BATHS OF THE SEVEN SAGES

Tiber

to the Sea

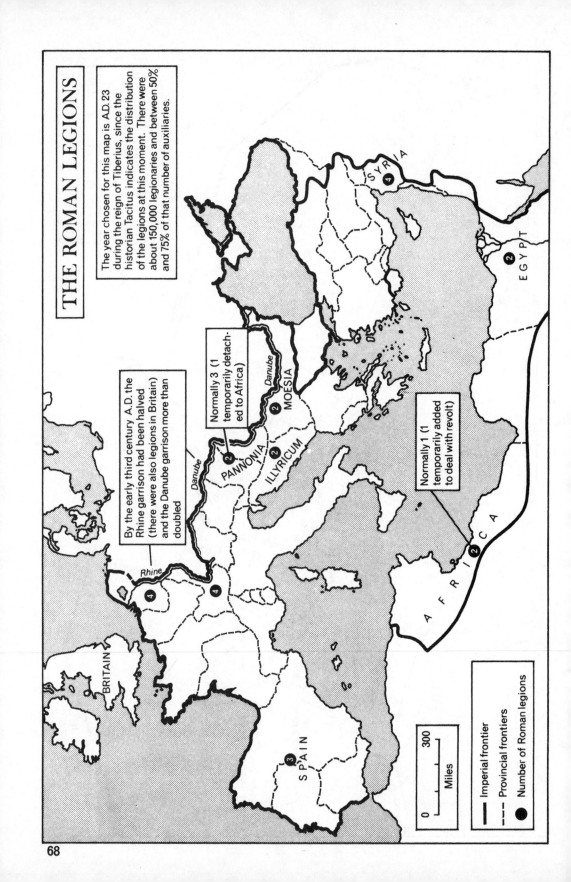

THE ROMAN LEGIONS

The year chosen for this map is A.D. 23 during the reign of Tiberius, since the historian Tacitus indicates the distribution of the legions at this moment. There were about 150,000 legionaries and between 50% and 75% of that number of auxiliaries.

By the early third century A.D. the Rhine garrison had been halved (there were also legions in Britain) and the Danube garrison more than doubled

Normally 3 (1 temporarily detach-ed to Africa)

Normally 1 (1 temporarily added to deal with revolt)

BRITAIN

Rhine

SPAIN

Danube

PANNONIA

Danube

ILLYRICUM

MOESIA

AFRICA

SYRIA

EGYPT

Imperial frontier
Provincial frontiers
Number of Roman legions

0   300
Miles

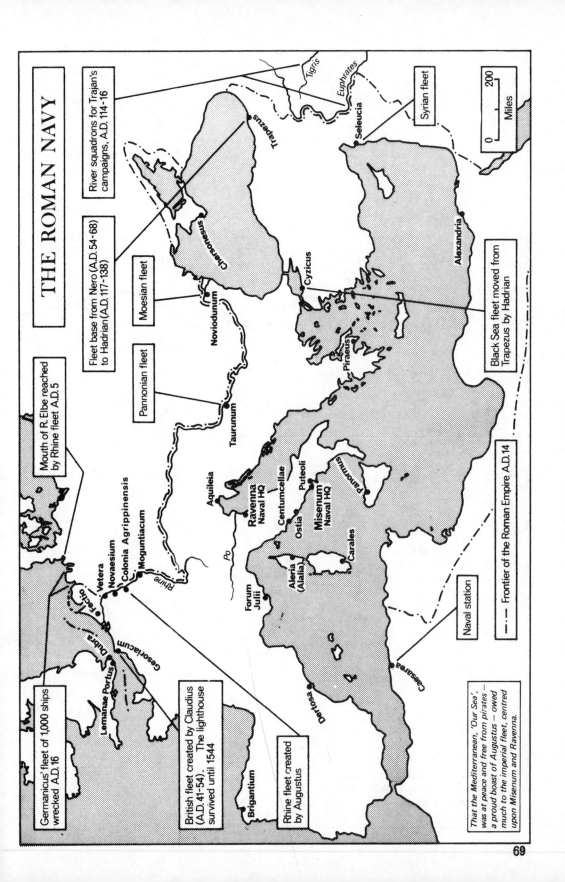

THE ROMAN NAVY

River squadrons for Trajan's campaigns, A.D. 114-16

Fleet base from Nero (A.D. 54-68) to Hadrian (A.D. 117-138)

Syrian fleet

Moesian fleet

Pannonian fleet

Black Sea fleet moved from Trapezus by Hadrian

Mouth of R. Elbe reached by Rhine fleet A.D. 5

Germanicus' fleet of 1,000 ships wrecked A.D. 16

British fleet created by Claudius (A.D. 41-54). The lighthouse survived until 1544

Rhine fleet created by Augustus

Naval station

Frontier of the Roman Empire A.D. 14

0   200
|_____|
Miles

That the Mediterranean, 'Our Sea', was at peace and free from pirates — a proud boast of Augustus — owed much to the imperial fleet, centred upon Misenum and Ravenna.

Tigris

Euphrates

Seleucia

Trapezus

Chersonesus

Cyzicus

Alexandria

Noviodunum

Piraeus

Taurunum

Aquileia

Ravenna Naval HQ

Centumcellae

Puteoli

Ostia

Misenum Naval HQ

Pannonius

Carales

Aleria (Alalia)

Forum Julii

Po

Rhine

Moguntiacum

Colonia Agrippinensis

Novaesium

Vetera

Gesoriacum

Rutupiae

Dubris

Lemanae Portus

Brigantium

Dertosa

Caesarea

69

BRITANNIA (AD 71)
(AD 59)
(AD 43-47)
Londinium

FREE GERMANY

LOWER GERMANY
Colonia Agrippinensis

Rhine

Moguntiacum

AGRI DECUMAT (83)

LUGDUNENSIS

UPPER GERMANY

RHAETIA

NORICUM

Danube

PANNONIA

UPPER

LOWER

GALLIA

Lugdunum

AQUITANIA

NARBONENSIS

Aquileia

ITALIA

ILLYRICUM

Nemausus

Adriatic Sea

TARRACONENSIS

Tarraco

Rome

HISPANIA

LUSITANIA

SARDINIA

BAETICA

Corduba

Gades

SICILY

Carthage

MAURETANIA (A.D.42)

AFRICA

- - - Frontier of Roman Empire A.D. 14
- · - · Frontier of Roman Empire A.D. 117
· · · · · Province boundaries

THE ROMAN EMPIRE FROM TIBERIUS (A.D.14-37) TO TRAJAN (98-117)

Trajan's expansion as far as the Persian Gulf came to nothing, since his successor Hadrian withdrew to the Euphrates again.

KINGDOM OF BOSPHORUS

Black Sea

Artaxata

ARMENIA MINOR (63)

ARMENIA (A.D.114)

SIA

THRACIA (A.D.44)

BITHYNIA-PONTUS

Ancyra

GALATIA

CAPPADOCIA (A.D.17)

ASSYRIA (A.D.115)

Tigris

MESOPOTAMIA (A.D.115)

Pergamum

ASIA

Aegean Sea

Corinth

Ephesus

PAMPHYLIA (43)

LYCIA

Antioch

SYRIA

Euphrates

Regions beyond Euphrates evacuated by Hadrian A.D.117

JUDAEA (A.D.6.44)

Alexandria

ARABIA (A.D.106)

CYRENE

EGYPT

Nile

0   200
Miles

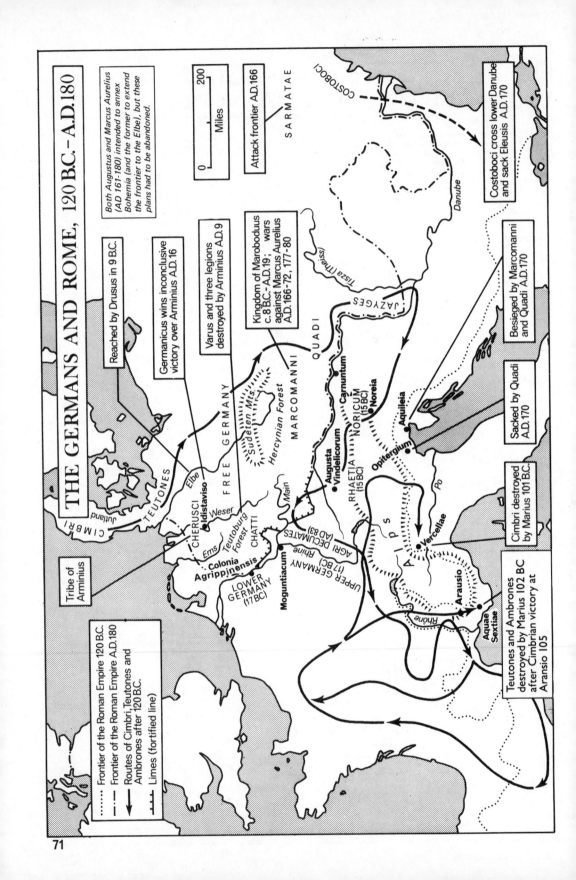

THE GERMANS AND ROME, 120 B.C. – A.D. 180

Both Augustus and Marcus Aurelius (AD 161-180) intended to annex Bohemia (and the former to extend the frontier to the Elbe), but these plans had to be abandoned.

Reached by Drusus in 9 B.C.

Germanicus wins inconclusive victory over Arminius A.D. 16

Varus and three legions destroyed by Arminius A.D. 9

Kingdom of Maroboduus c. 8 B.C.–A.D. 19; wars against Marcus Aurelius A.D. 166-72, 177-80

Attack frontier A.D. 166

Costoboci cross lower Danube and sack Eleusis A.D. 170

Besieged by Marcomanni and Quadi A.D. 170

Sacked by Quadi A.D. 170

Cimbri destroyed by Marius 101 B.C.

Teutones and Ambrones destroyed by Marius 102 BC after Cimbrian victory at Aransio 105

Tribe of Arminius

.... Frontier of the Roman Empire 120 B.C.
– – – Frontier of the Roman Empire A.D. 180
→ Routes of Cimbri, Teutones and Ambrones after 120 B.C.
⊢⊢⊢ Limes (fortified line)

0   200
Miles

SARMATAE

COSTOBOCI

Danube

Tisza (Theiss)

JAZYGES

QUADI

MARCOMANNI

Hercynian Forest

Sudeten Mts.

FREE GERMANY

TEUTONES

CIMBRI

Jutland

Elbe

Idistaviso

CHERUSCI

Weser

Ems

Teutoburg Forest

CHATTI

Colonia
Agrippinensis

LOWER
GERMANY
(17BC)

Moguntiacum

Rhine

UPPER GERMANY
(17BC)

AGRI DECUMATES
(AD 83)

Main

Augusta
Vindelicorum

RHAETIA
(15BC)

Carnuntum

NORICUM
(15BC)

Noreia

Opitergium

Aquileia

A L P S

Po

Vercellae

Rhone

Arausio

Aquae
Sextiae

71

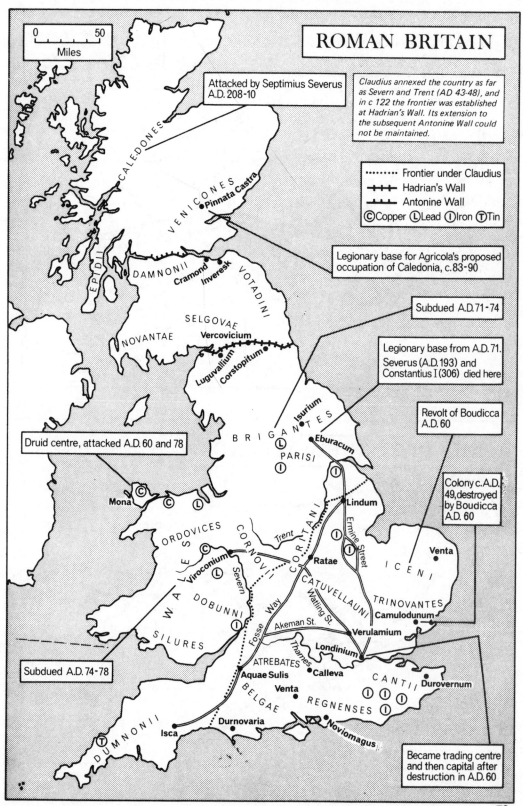

ROMAN BRITAIN

Attacked by Septimius Severus
A.D. 208-10

Claudius annexed the country as far as Severn and Trent (AD 43-48), and in c 122 the frontier was established at Hadrian's Wall. Its extension to the subsequent Antonine Wall could not be maintained.

········· Frontier under Claudius
╈╈╈ Hadrian's Wall
╈╈╈ Antonine Wall
ⒸCopper ⓁLead ⒾIron ⓉTin

Legionary base for Agricola's proposed occupation of Caledonia, c.83-90

Subdued A.D. 71-74

Legionary base from A.D. 71. Severus (A.D. 193) and Constantius I (306) died here

Revolt of Boudicca A.D. 60

Druid centre, attacked A.D. 60 and 78

Colony c.A.D. 49, destroyed by Boudicca A.D. 60

Subdued A.D. 74-78

Became trading centre and then capital after destruction in A.D. 60

0 ___ 50
Miles

CALEDONES

VENICONES
Pinnata Castra

EPIDII

DAMNONII
Cramond · Invenesk

VOTADINI

SELGOVAE
Vercovicium

NOVANTAE

Luguvallium · Corstopitum

BRIGANTES
Isurium
ⓁⒾ
Eburacum
PARISI

Mona Ⓒ Ⓒ Ⓛ

ORDOVICES Ⓒ
Viroconium Ⓛ
CORNOVII
Trent
Lindum
ⒾⒾ
Ermine Street

Ratae
CORITANI
Venta
ICENI

WALES
Severn

DOBUNNI
Ⓘ
Fosse Way
Akeman St.
CATUVELLAUNI
Watling St.
TRINOVANTES
Camulodunum

SILURES
Verulamium

ATREBATES
Londinium
Thames
Calleva
Aquae Sulis
Venta
BELGAE
CANTII
Durovernum

DUMNONII
Isca
Durnovaria
REGNENSES
Ⓘ Ⓘ Ⓘ
Ⓘ
Noviomagus

Ⓣ

72

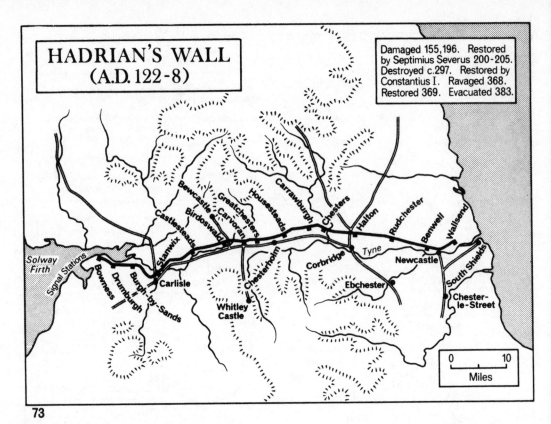

HADRIAN'S WALL
(A.D. 122-8)

Damaged 155, 196. Restored by Septimius Severus 200-205. Destroyed c.297. Restored by Constantius I. Ravaged 368. Restored 369. Evacuated 383.

Bewcastle

Castlesteads
Birdoswald
Greatchesters
Carvoran
Housesteads
Carrawburgh
Chesters
Halton
Rudchester
Benwell
Wallsend

Solway Firth

Signal Stations

Bowness
Drumburgh
Burgh-by-Sands
Stanwix
Carlisle
Chesterholm
Corbridge
Tyne
Newcastle
South Shields

Whitley Castle
Ebchester
Chester-le-Street

0   10
Miles

73

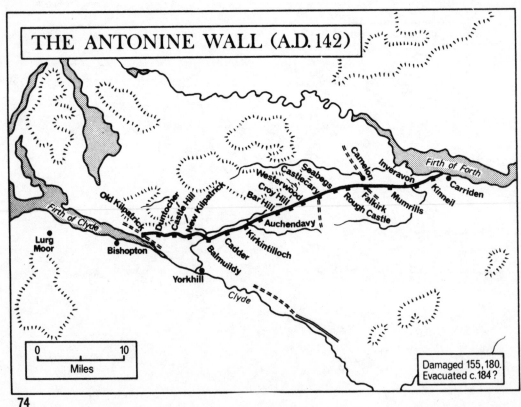

THE ANTONINE WALL (A.D. 142)

Firth of Forth

Camelon
Inveravon
Carriden
Kinneil
Mumrills
Falkirk
Rough Castle
Seabegs
Castlecary
Westerwood
Croy Hill
Bar Hill
Auchendavy

Old Kilpatrick
Duntocher
Castle Hill
New Kilpatrick
Kirkintilloch
Cadder
Balmuildy

Firth of Clyde

Lurg Moor
Bishopton
Yorkhill
Clyde

0   10
Miles

Damaged 155, 180. Evacuated c.184?

74

THE WORLD ACCORDING TO PTOLEMY, c. A.D. 150

The Geography of Claudius Ptolemaeus of Alexandria, including an atlas, showed awareness of the existence of China, but not of its shape.

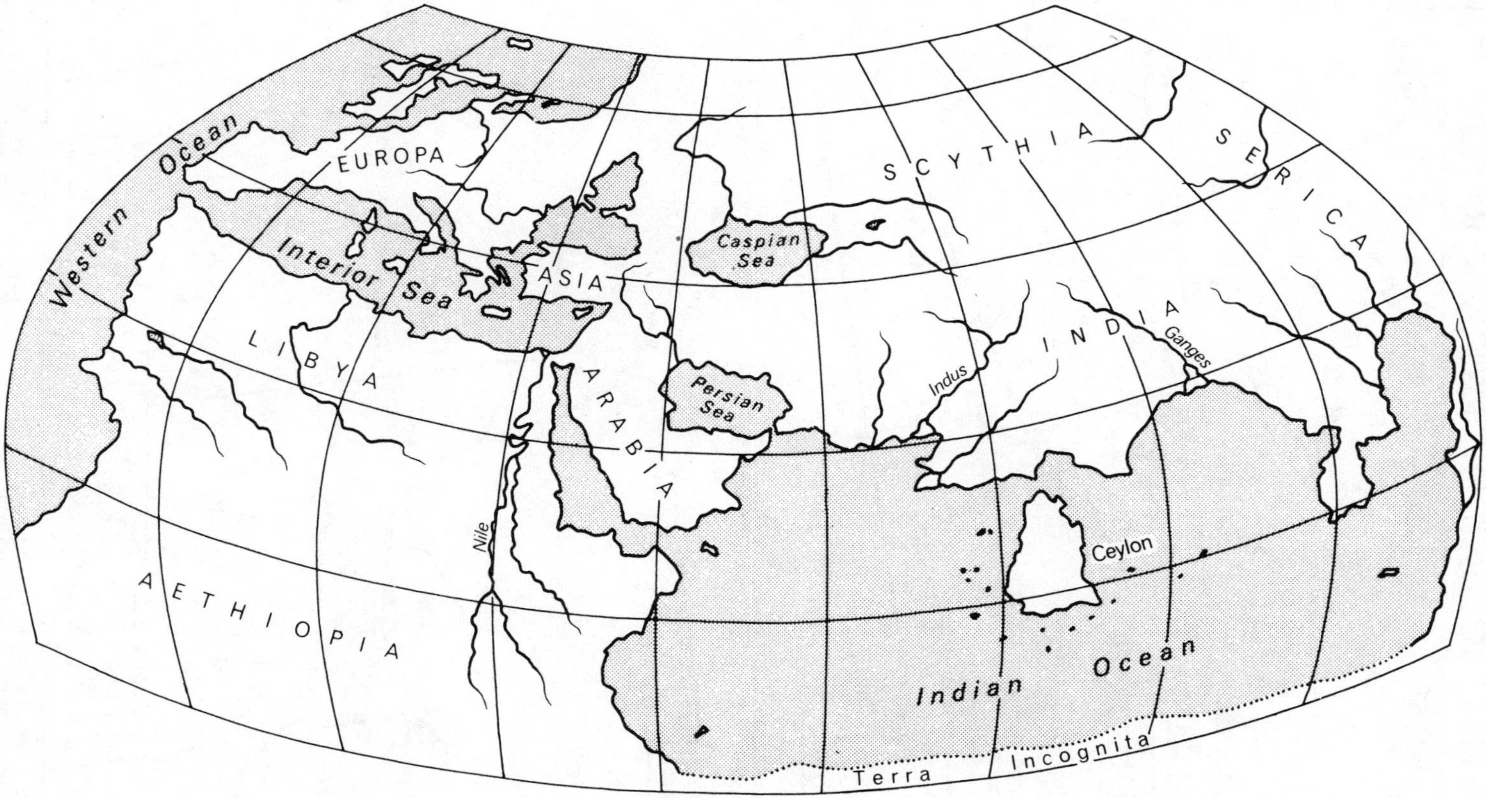

SERICA

SCYTHIA

INDIA

Ganges

Indus

Ceylon

Indian Ocean

Terra Incognita

Caspian Sea

Persian Sea

ARABIA

ASIA

EUROPA

Interior Sea

LIBYA

Nile

AETHIOPIA

Western Ocean

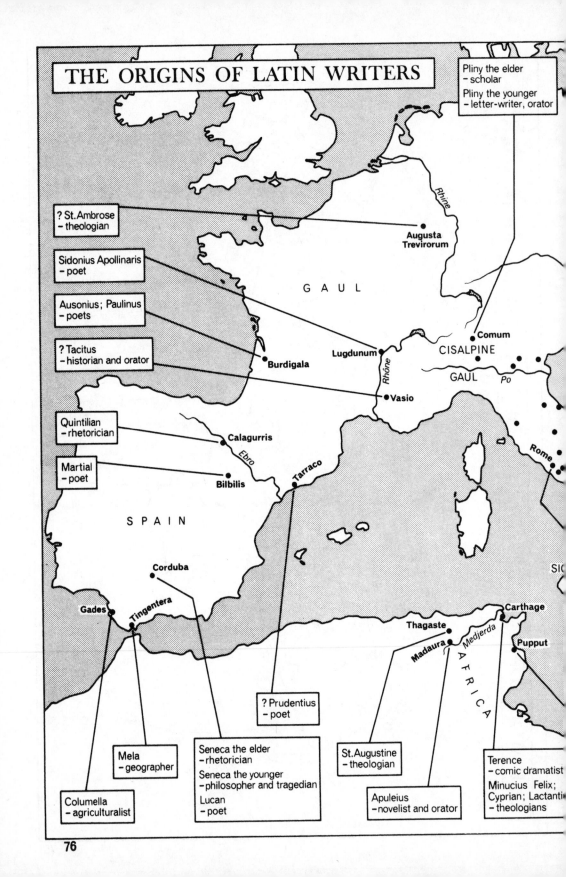

THE ORIGINS OF LATIN WRITERS

Pliny the elder
– scholar
Pliny the younger
– letter-writer, orator

? St.Ambrose
– theologian

Sidonius Apollinaris
– poet

Ausonius; Paulinus
– poets

? Tacitus
– historian and orator

Quintilian
– rhetorician

Martial
– poet

GAUL

Augusta
Trevirorum

Comum
CISALPINE
GAUL   Po

Lugdunum

Rhône

Burdigala

Vasio

Calagurris

Ebro

Tarraco

Bilbilis

Rome

SPAIN

Corduba

Gades   Tingentera

Carthage

Thagaste

Madaura   Medjerda

Pupput

AFRICA

SIC

? Prudentius
– poet

Mela
– geographer

Seneca the elder
– rhetorician
Seneca the younger
– philosopher and tragedian
Lucan
– poet

St.Augustine
– theologian

Terence
– comic dramatist

Minucius Felix;
Cyprian; Lactanti
– theologians

Columella
– agriculturalist

Apuleius
–novelist and orator

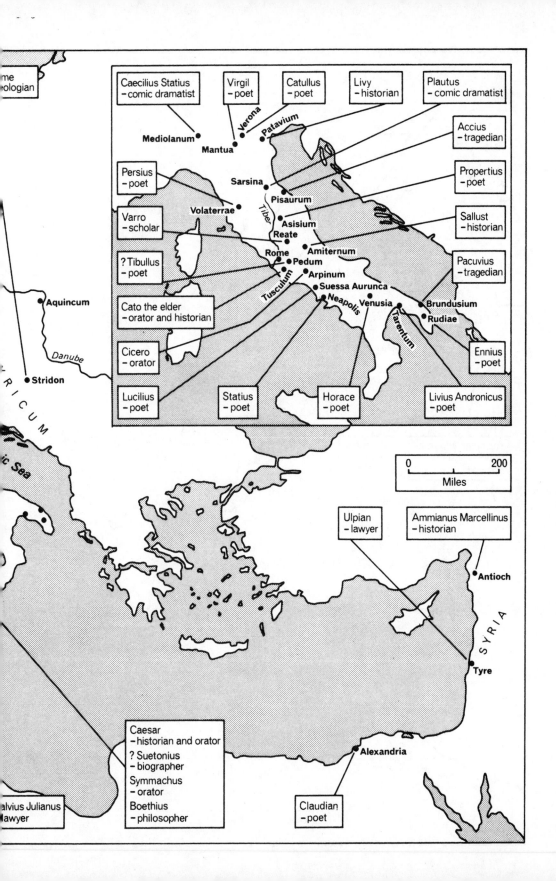

Caecilius Statius
– comic dramatist

Virgil
– poet

Catullus
– poet

Livy
– historian

Plautus
– comic dramatist

Accius
– tragedian

Persius
– poet

Propertius
– poet

Varro
– scholar

Sallust
– historian

?Tibullus
– poet

Pacuvius
– tragedian

Cato the elder
– orator and historian

Cicero
– orator

Ennius
– poet

Lucilius
– poet

Statius
– poet

Horace
– poet

Livius Andronicus
– poet

Verona
Patavium
Mediolanum
Mantua
Sarsina
Pisaurum
Volaterrae
Asisium
Tiber
Reate
Rome
Amiternum
Pedum
Arpinum
Tusculum
Suessa Aurunca
Neapolis
Venusia
Brundusium
Tarentum
Rudiae

me
ologian

Aquincum

Danube

RICUM

Stridon

ic Sea

0   200
Miles

Ulpian
– lawyer

Ammianus Marcellinus
– historian

Antioch

SYRIA

Tyre

Caesar
– historian and orator

?Suetonius
– biographer

Symmachus
– orator

Boethius
– philosopher

Claudian
– poet

Alexandria

alvius Julianus
lawyer

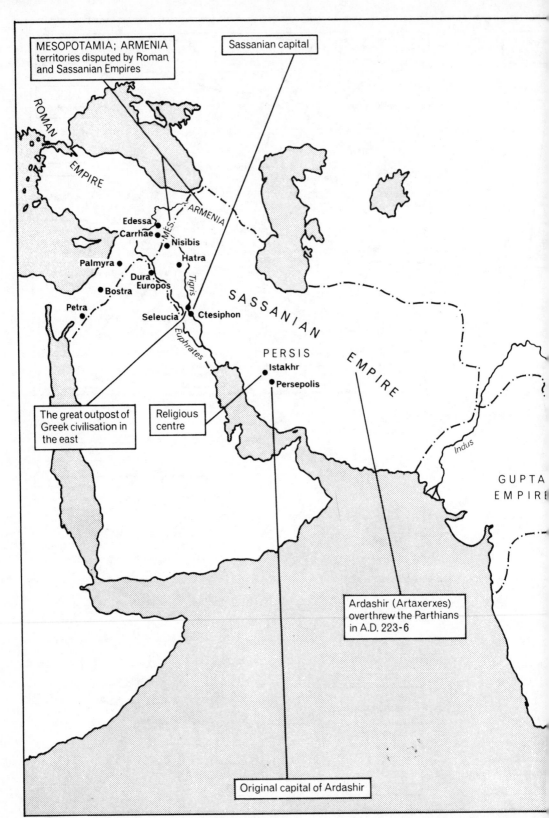

MESOPOTAMIA; ARMENIA
territories disputed by Roman
and Sassanian Empires

Sassanian capital

ROMAN

EMPIRE

ARMENIA

Edessa
Carrhae
MES.
Nisibis
Hatra
Palmyra
Dura
Europos
Bostra
Tigris
SASSANIAN
Petra
Seleucia
Ctesiphon
EMPIRE
Euphrates
PERSIS
Istakhr
Persepolis
Indus

The great outpost of
Greek civilisation in
the east

Religious
centre

GUPTA
EMPIRE

Ardashir (Artaxerxes)
overthrew the Parthians
in A.D. 223-6

Original capital of Ardashir

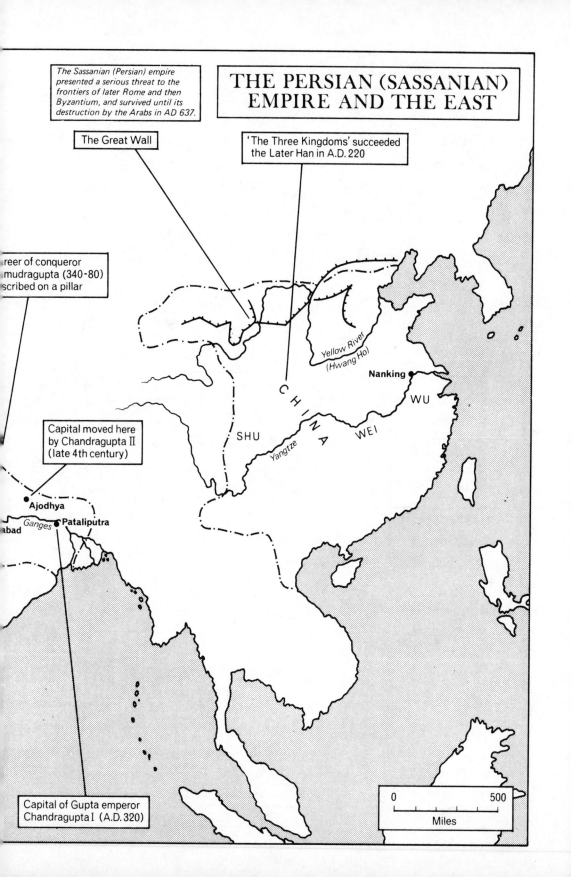

The Sassanian (Persian) empire presented a serious threat to the frontiers of later Rome and then Byzantium, and survived until its destruction by the Arabs in AD 637.

THE PERSIAN (SASSANIAN) EMPIRE AND THE EAST

The Great Wall

'The Three Kingdoms' succeeded the Later Han in A.D. 220

reer of conqueror mudragupta (340-80) scribed on a pillar

Yellow River (Hwang Ho)

Nanking

C H I N A

WU

SHU

WEI

Yangtze

Capital moved here by Chandragupta II (late 4th century)

Ajodhya

Ganges **Pataliputra**

abad

Capital of Gupta emperor Chandragupta I (A.D. 320)

0   500

Miles

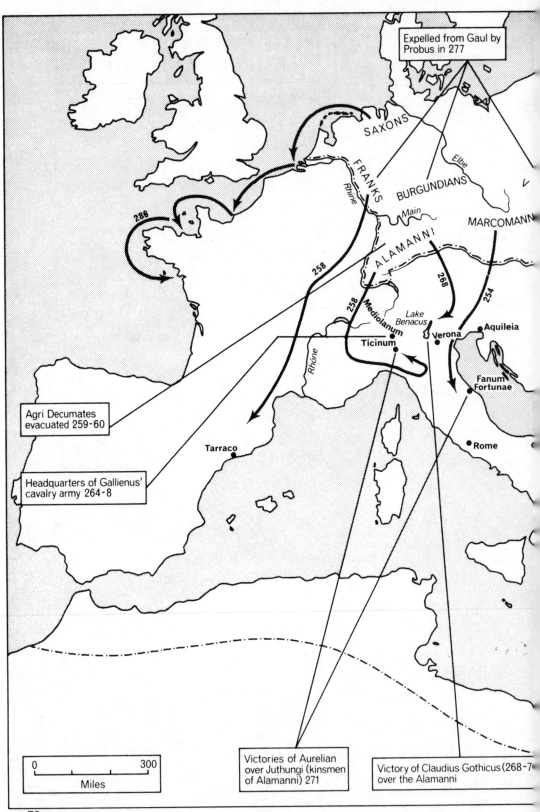

Expelled from Gaul by
Probus in 277

SAXONS

Elbe

FRANKS

Rhine

BURGUNDIANS

Main

MARCOMANNI

286

ALAMANNI

258

258

268

254

Mediolanum

Lake
Benacus

Verona

Aquileia

Ticinum

Rhône

Fanum
Fortunae

Agri Decumates
evacuated 259-60

Tarraco

Rome

Headquarters of Gallienus'
cavalry army 264-8

Victories of Aurelian
over Juthungi (kinsmen
of Alamanni) 271

Victory of Claudius Gothicus (268-7
over the Alamanni

0   300

Miles

GERMAN INVASIONS IN THE THIRD CENTURY A.D.

From the 230s until the 260s the Germans burst over the frontiers with ever increasing force, but then the dissolution of the empire was prevented by Gallienus, Claudius II Gothicus, Aurelian and Probus.

Evacuated c.271

First crossed the Danube under Severus Alexander (222-35)

King lends fleet to raiders 254

Decius fell to Goths 251

Overrun by Goths 256

Dnieper

Dniester

EAST GOTHS

HERULI

Cimmerian Bosphorus

Panticapaeum

DACIA

WEST GOTHS

ube

Abrittus

264

269

Marcianopolis

Black Sea

Trapezus

SASSANIAN EMPIRE

incum

Naïssus

Philippopolis

Byzantium

Chalcedon

BITHYNIA

Thessalonica

Pessinus

Ephesus

Sparta

Victory of Gallienus over Goths 268

Captured by Goths from Decius (249-51)

Sacked by Goths in 253

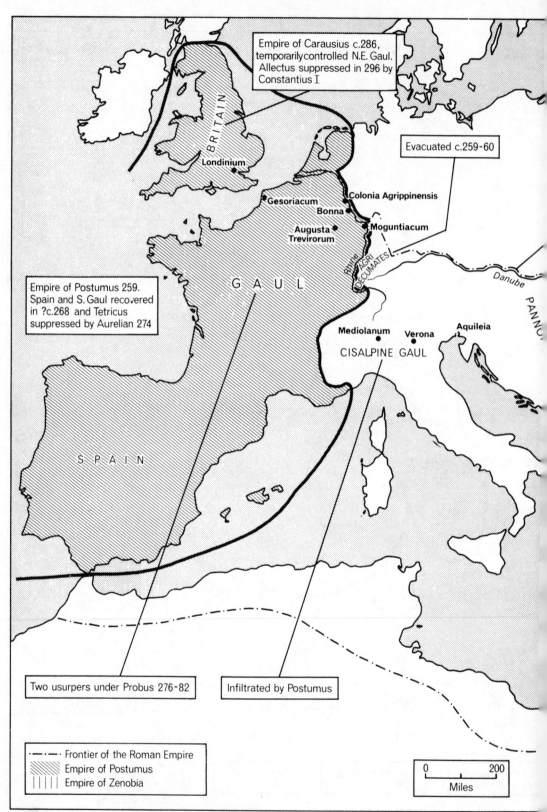

Empire of Carausius c.286, temporarily controlled N.E. Gaul. Allectus suppressed in 296 by Constantius I

Evacuated c.259-60

Empire of Postumus 259. Spain and S. Gaul recovered in ?c.268 and Tetricus suppressed by Aurelian 274

BRITAIN

Londinium

Gesoriacum

Colonia Agrippinensis

Bonna

Augusta Treverorum

Moguntiacum

RHINE

AGRI DECUMATES

Danube

PANNO.

G A U L

Mediolanum

Verona

Aquileia

CISALPINE GAUL

S P A I N

Two usurpers under Probus 276-82

Infiltrated by Postumus

Frontier of the Roman Empire

Empire of Postumus

Empire of Zenobia

0   200

Miles

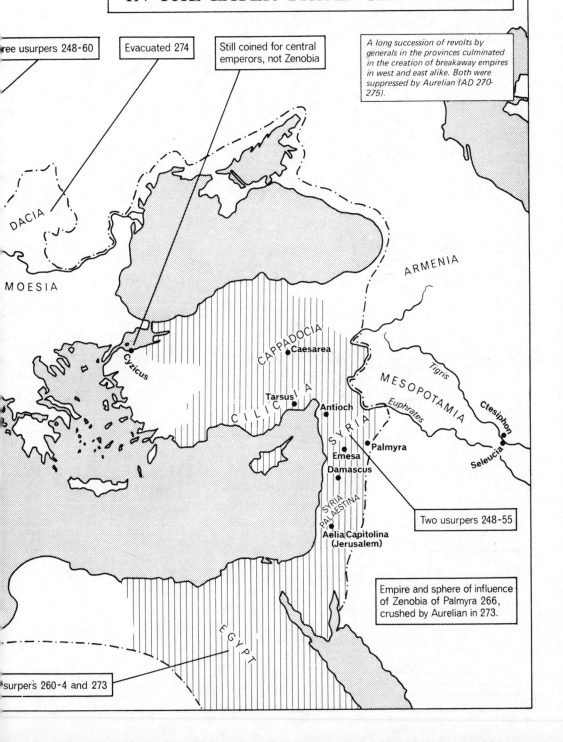

THE BREAKDOWN AND RECOVERY OF THE ROMAN EMPIRE IN THE LATER THIRD CENTURY A.D.

ree usurpers 248-60

Evacuated 274

Still coined for central emperors, not Zenobia

A long succession of revolts by generals in the provinces culminated in the creation of breakaway empires in west and east alike. Both were suppressed by Aurelian (AD 270-275).

DACIA

MOESIA

ARMENIA

CAPPADOCIA

Caesarea

Cyzicus

Tigris

MESOPOTAMIA

C I L I C I A

Tarsus

Euphrates

Ctesiphon

Antioch

S Y R I A

Palmyra

Seleucia

Emesa

Damascus

Two usurpers 248-55

SYRIA PALAESTINA

Aelia Capitolina (Jerusalem)

Empire and sphere of influence of Zenobia of Palmyra 266, crushed by Aurelian in 273.

E G Y P T

surpers 260-4 and 273

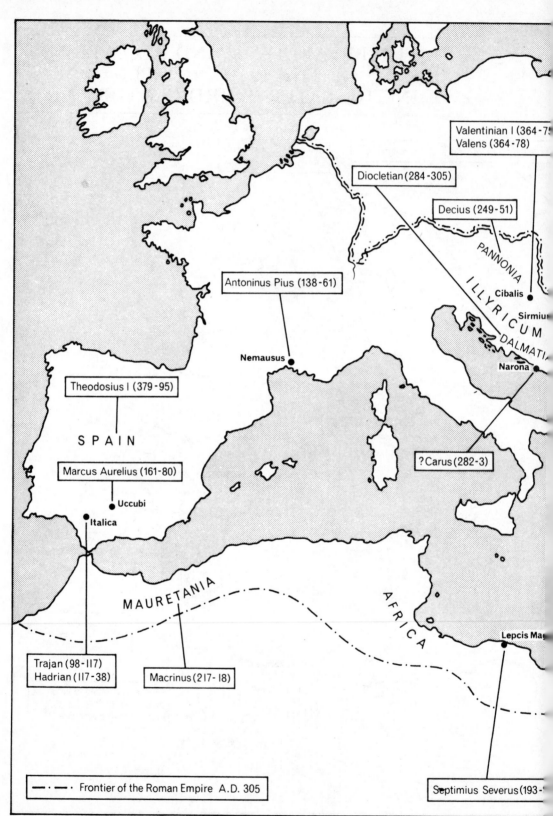

Valentinian I (364-7[5])
Valens (364-78)

Diocletian (284-305)

Decius (249-51)

PANNONIA

ILLYRICUM

Cibalis

Sirmiu[m]

DALMATIA

Antoninus Pius (138-61)

Narona

Nemausus

Theodosius I (379-95)

SPAIN

?Carus (282-3)

Marcus Aurelius (161-80)

Uccubi

Italica

MAURETANIA

AFRICA

Lepcis Ma[gna]

Trajan (98-117)
Hadrian (117-38)

Macrinus (217-18)

Septimius Severus (193-[ )

—·—·— Frontier of the Roman Empire A.D. 305

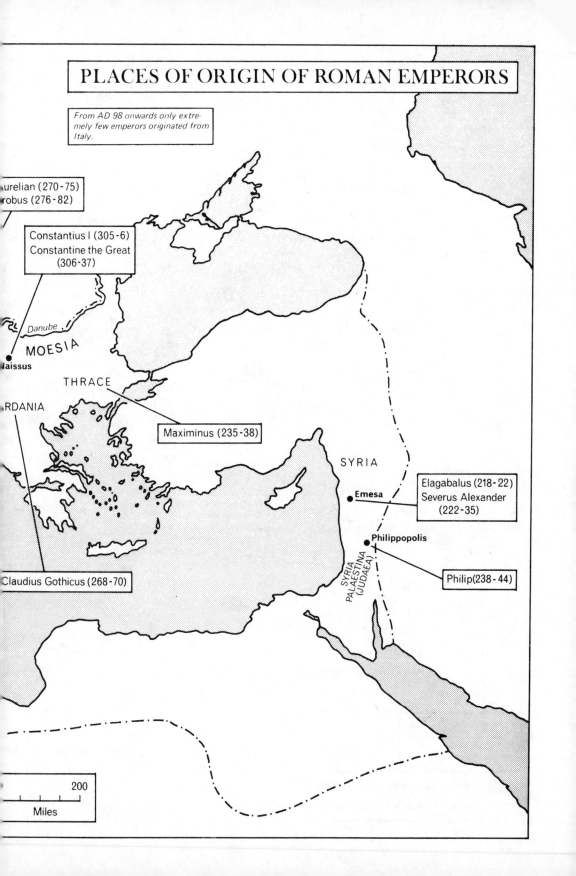

PLACES OF ORIGIN OF ROMAN EMPERORS

From AD 98 onwards only extremely few emperors originated from Italy.

Aurelian (270-75)
Probus (276-82)

Constantius I (305-6)
Constantine the Great
(306-37)

Danube

MOESIA

Naissus

THRACE

DARDANIA

Maximinus (235-38)

SYRIA

Elagabalus (218-22)
Severus Alexander
(222-35)

Emesa

Philippopolis

SYRIA
PALAESTINA
(JUDAEA)

Philip (238-44)

Claudius Gothicus (268-70)

200

Miles

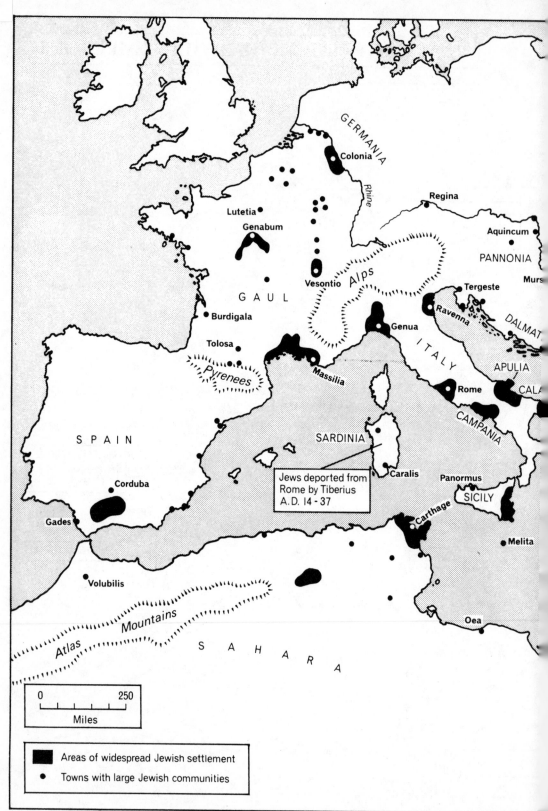

Jews deported from
Rome by Tiberius
A.D. 14 - 37

Areas of widespread Jewish settlement
Towns with large Jewish communities

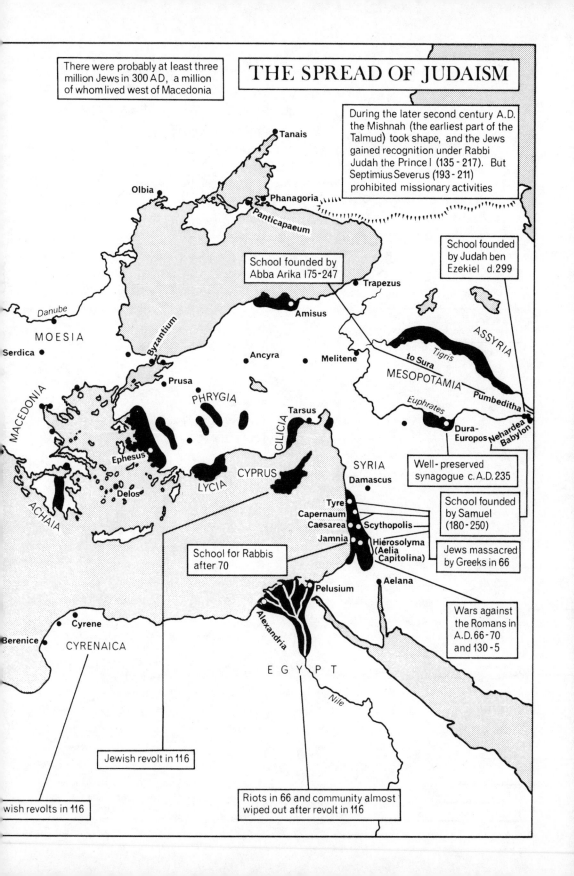

THE SPREAD OF JUDAISM

There were probably at least three million Jews in 300 AD, a million of whom lived west of Macedonia

During the later second century A.D. the Mishnah (the earliest part of the Talmud) took shape, and the Jews gained recognition under Rabbi Judah the Prince I (135-217). But Septimius Severus (193-211) prohibited missionary activities

School founded by Judah ben Ezekiel d.299

School founded by Abba Arika 175-247

Well-preserved synagogue c.A.D.235

School founded by Samuel (180-250)

School for Rabbis after 70

Jews massacred by Greeks in 66

Wars against the Romans in A.D.66-70 and 130-5

Jewish revolt in 116

Riots in 66 and community almost wiped out after revolt in 116

wish revolts in 116

Tanais

Olbia

Phanagoria

Panticapaeum

Danube

MOESIA

Serdica

Byzantium

Prusa

Ancyra

Melitene

PHRYGIA

Tarsus

CILICIA

Ephesus

Delos

CYPRUS

LYCIA

ACHAIA

MACEDONIA

Trapezus

Amisus

to Sura

Tigris

ASSYRIA

MESOPOTAMIA

Euphrates

Pumbeditha

Dura-Europos

Nehardea

Babylon

SYRIA

Damascus

Tyre

Capernaum

Caesarea

Scythopolis

Jamnia

Hierosolyma (Aelia Capitolina)

Pelusium

Aelana

Cyrene

Berenice

CYRENAICA

Alexandria

E G Y P T

Nile

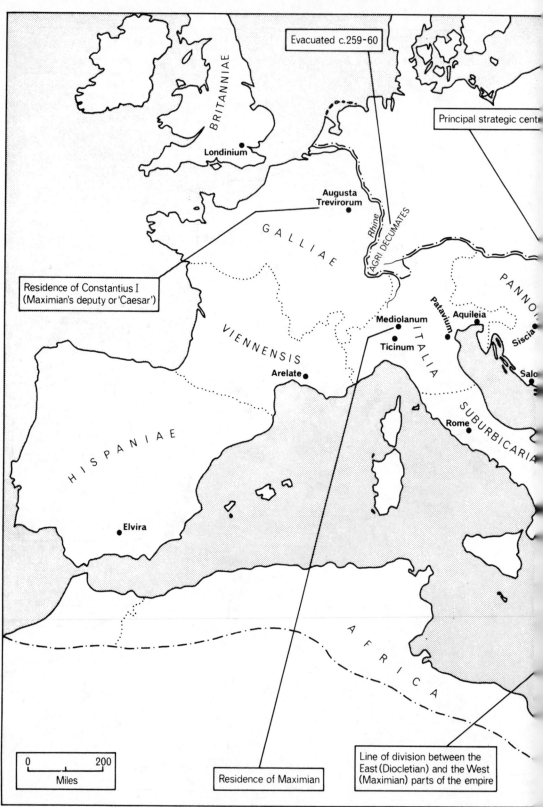

Evacuated c.259-60

Principal strategic cent[r]

Residence of Constantius I
(Maximian's deputy or 'Caesar')

BRITANNIAE

Londinium

Augusta
Trevirorum

G A L L I A E

Rhine

AGRI DECUMATES

P A N N O[N]

Patavium

Aquileia

Siscia

Mediolanum

V I E N N E N S I S

Ticinum

I T A L I A

Salo[na]

Arelate

Rome

S U B U R B I C A R I A

H I S P A N I A E

Elvira

A F R I C A

0   200

Miles

Residence of Maximian

Line of division between the
East (Diocletian) and the West
(Maximian) parts of the empire

THE ROMAN EMPIRE UNDER DIOCLETIAN AND MAXIMIAN A.D. 284/6-305

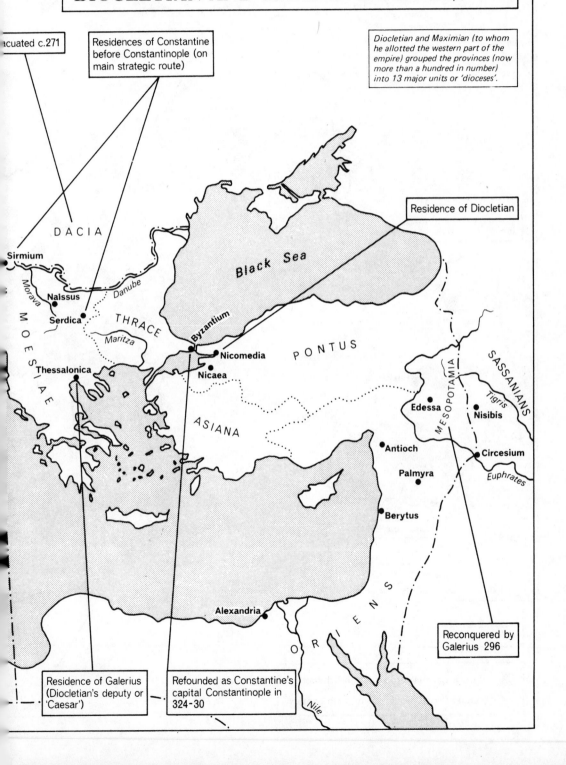

acuated c.271

Residences of Constantine before Constantinople (on main strategic route)

Diocletian and Maximian (to whom he allotted the western part of the empire) grouped the provinces (now more than a hundred in number) into 13 major units or 'dioceses'.

Residence of Diocletian

DACIA

Sirmium

Morava

Naissus

Serdica

Danube

THRACE

Maritza

Byzantium

Nicomedia

Nicaea

PONTUS

Black Sea

M O E S I A E

Thessalonica

ASIANA

SASSANIANS

MESOPOTAMIA

Tigris

Edessa

Nisibis

Antioch

Circesium

Palmyra

Euphrates

Berytus

O R I E N S

Alexandria

Nile

Reconquered by Galerius 296

Residence of Galerius (Diocletian's deputy or 'Caesar')

Refounded as Constantine's capital Constantinople in 324-30

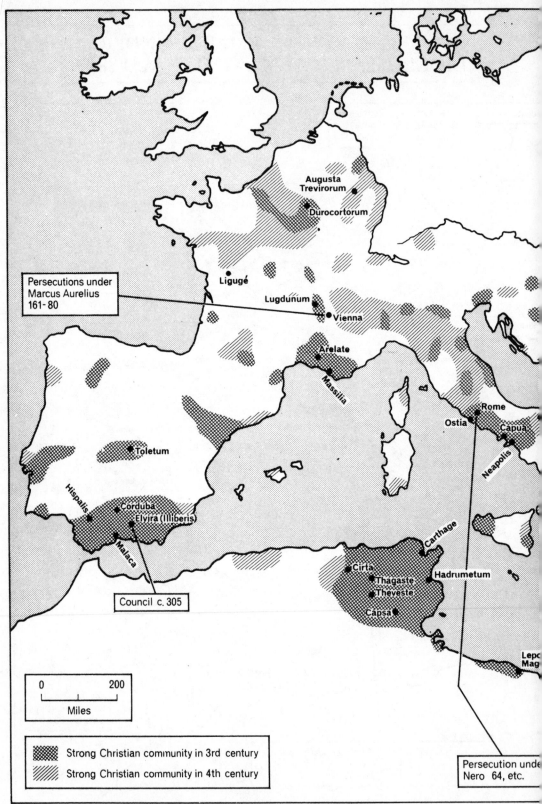

Persecutions under
Marcus Aurelius
161-80

Council c. 305

Augusta
Trevirorum

Durocortorum

Ligugé

Lugdunum

Vienna

Arelate

Massilia

Toletum

Hispalis

Corduba
Elvira (Illiberis)

Malaca

Rome

Ostia

Capua

Neapolis

Carthage

Cirta

Thagaste
Theveste

Hadrumetum

Capsa

Lepc
Mag

0	200

Miles

Strong Christian community in 3rd century

Strong Christian community in 4th century

Persecution unde
Nero 64, etc.

THE SPREAD OF CHRISTIANITY

*After the Edict of Milan (AD 313)
had introduced universal religious
tolerance, Christianity gradually
became the official religion under
Constantine the Great (d 337).*

☐ THE SEVEN CHURCHES OF ASIA

1 Pergamum   5 Philadelphia
2 Thyatira   6 Ephesus
3 Sardis   7 Laodicea
4 Smyrna

Mission of Ulfila
d. 383

WEST GOTHS

Council 324

Byzantium
(Constantinople)
Nicaea

ARMENIA

Converted c.280

Prusa

Ancyra

Samosata

Edessa

Arbela

Nisibis

Thessalonica

Iconium

Tarsus

Antioch

First bishop
consecrated c.200

Corinth

Perga

Sparta

Rhodes

Salamis

CYPRUS

Citium

CRETE

Cnossus

Sidon

Tyre

Bostra

Gortyna

Caesarea

Monastery of
St. Hilarion
(early 4th century)

Gaza

Jerusalem
Bethlehem

Cyrene

83 executions
recorded in
Gt. Persecutions
303-13

Barca

Berenice

Alexandria

Memphis

E

Population may have been
50% Christian by 300

G

Oxyrhynchus

Y

Hermopolis

P

Centre of
monasticism

THEBAID

T

Kufra
Oasis

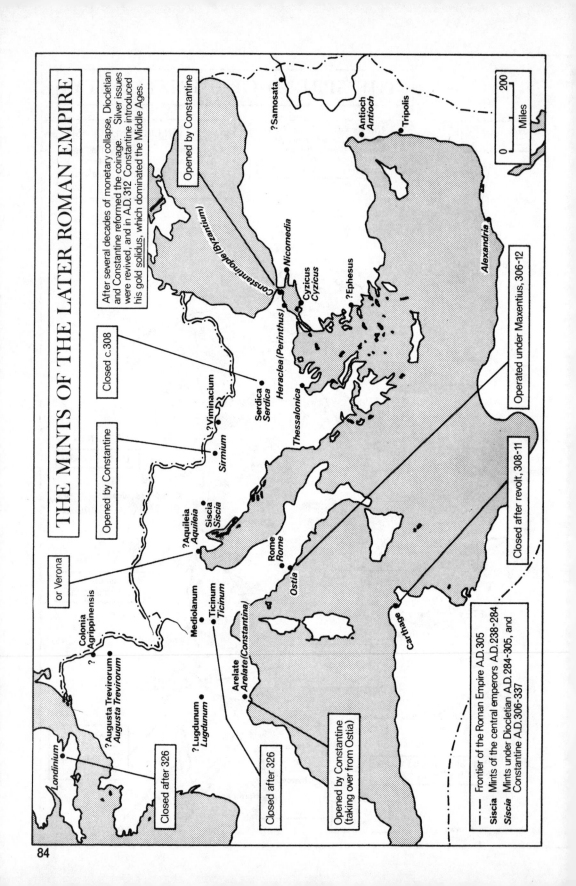

THE MINTS OF THE LATER ROMAN EMPIRE

After several decades of monetary collapse, Diocletian and Constantine reformed the coinage. Silver issues were revived, and in A.D. 312 Constantine introduced his gold solidus, which dominated the Middle Ages.

Opened by Constantine

Closed c.308

Opened by Constantine

or Verona

Closed after 326

Closed after 326

Opened by Constantine
(taking over from Ostia)

Operated under Maxentius, 306-12

Closed after revolt, 308-11

Londinium

?Augusta Trevirorum
Augusta Trevirorum

Colonia
Agrippinensis
?

?Lugdunum
Lugdunum

Mediolanum

Ticinum
Ticinum

Arelate *(Constantina)*
Arelate (Constantina)

?Aquileia
Aquileia

Siscia
Siscia

Sirmium

?Viminacium

Serdica
Serdica

Rome
Rome

Ostia

Carthage

Thessalonica

Heraclea *(Perinthus)*

Constantinople *(Byzantium)*

Nicomedia

Cyzicus
Cyzicus

?Ephesus

?Samosata

Antioch
Antioch

Tripolis

Alexandria

0   200
Miles

— · — Frontier of the Roman Empire A.D.305
Siscia Mints of the central emperors A.D.238-284
Siscia Mints under Diocletian A.D.284-305, and
Constantine A.D.306-337

84

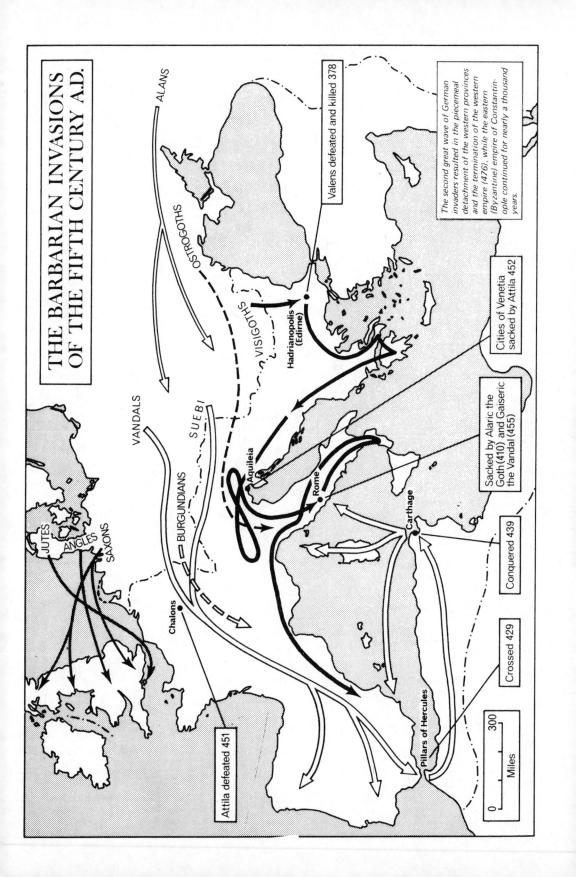

THE BARBARIAN INVASIONS OF THE FIFTH CENTURY A.D.

ALANS

OSTROGOTHS

VISIGOTHS

VANDALS

SUEBI

BURGUNDIANS

JUTES

ANGLES

SAXONS

Chalons

Aquileia

Rome

Carthage

Hadrianopolis (Edirne)

Pillars of Hercules

Valens defeated and killed 378

Cities of Venetia sacked by Attila 452

Sacked by Alaric the Goth (410) and Gaiseric the Vandal (455)

Conquered 439

Crossed 429

Attila defeated 451

The second great wave of German invaders resulted in the piecemeal detachment of the western provinces and the termination of the western empire (476), while the eastern (Byzantine) empire of Constantinople continued for nearly a thousand years.

0   300
Miles

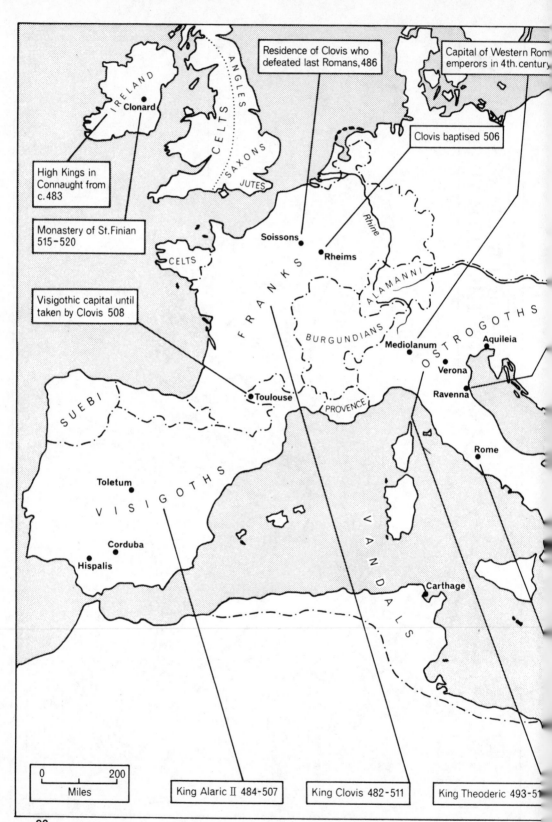

IRELAND

CELTS

ANGLES

SAXONS

JUTES

Clonard

High Kings in Connaught from c.483

Monastery of St.Finian 515–520

Residence of Clovis who defeated last Romans, 486

Capital of Western Rom emperors in 4th. century

Clovis baptised 506

CELTS

FRANKS

Rhine

ALAMANNI

Soissons

Rheims

Visigothic capital until taken by Clovis 508

BURGUNDIANS

OSTROGOTHS

Aquileia

Mediolanum

Verona

Ravenna

SUEBI

Toulouse

PROVENCE

Rome

Toletum

VISIGOTHS

V A N D A L S

Corduba

Hispalis

Carthage

0   200
Miles

King Alaric II 484–507

King Clovis 482–511

King Theoderic 493–51

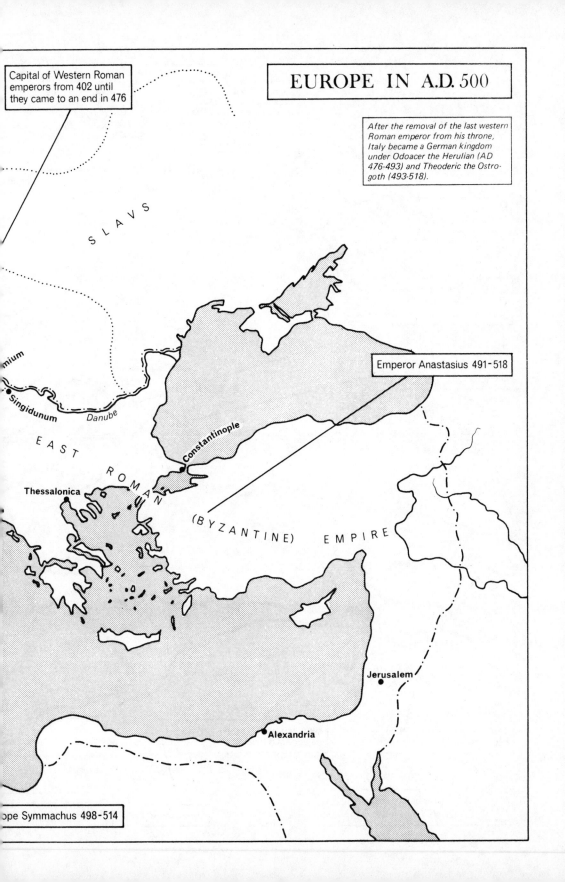

EUROPE IN A.D. 500

Capital of Western Roman emperors from 402 until they came to an end in 476

After the removal of the last western Roman emperor from his throne, Italy became a German kingdom under Odoacer the Herulian (AD 476-493) and Theoderic the Ostrogoth (493-518).

SLAVS

Emperor Anastasius 491-518

...mium

Singidunum   Danube

E A S T

R O M A N

Constantinople

Thessalonica

(B Y Z A N T I N E)   E M P I R E

Jerusalem

Alexandria

ope Symmachus 498-514

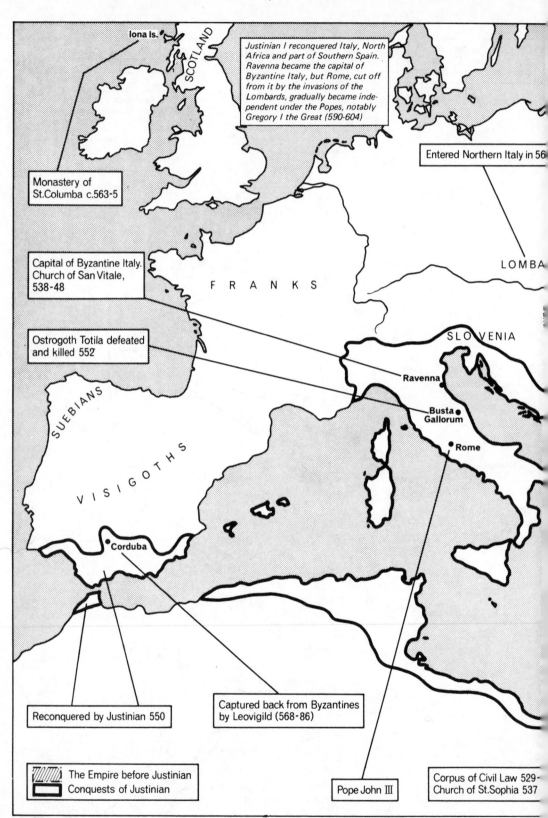

Iona Is.

SCOTLAND

Justinian I reconquered Italy, North
Africa and part of Southern Spain.
Ravenna became the capital of
Byzantine Italy, but Rome, cut off
from it by the invasions of the
Lombards, gradually became inde-
pendent under the Popes, notably
Gregory I the Great (590-604)

Entered Northern Italy in 56

Monastery of
St.Columba c.563-5

LOMBA

F R A N K S

Capital of Byzantine Italy.
Church of San Vitale,
538-48

SLO VENIA

Ostrogoth Totila defeated
and killed 552

Ravenna

Busta
Gallorum

Rome

SUEBIANS

V I S I G O T H S

Corduba

Reconquered by Justinian 550

Captured back from Byzantines
by Leovigild (568-86)

The Empire before Justinian
Conquests of Justinian

Pope John III

Corpus of Civil Law 529-
Church of St.Sophia 537

THE BYZANTINE EMPIRE OF JUSTINIAN I
(A.D. 527-65)

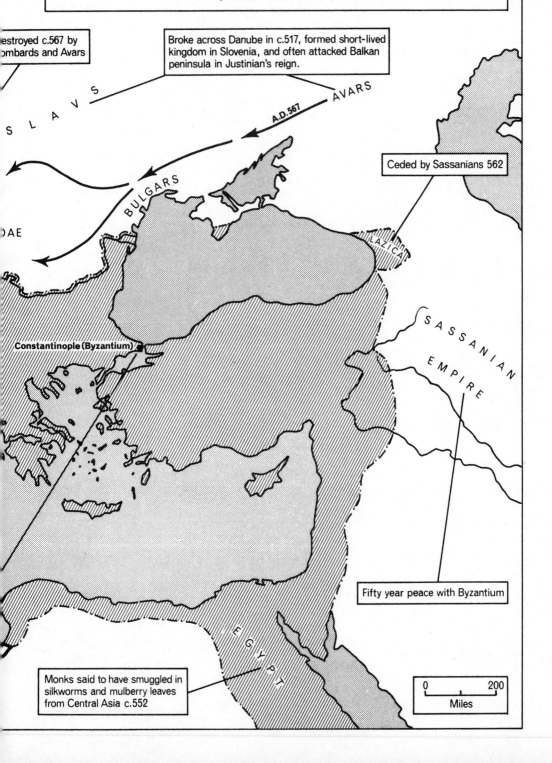

estroyed c.567 by
ombards and Avars

Broke across Danube in c.517, formed short-lived
kingdom in Slovenia, and often attacked Balkan
peninsula in Justinian's reign.

S L A V S

AVARS

A.D. 567

BULGARS

Ceded by Sassanians 562

DAE

LAZICA

S A S S A N I A N

E M P I R E

Constantinople (Byzantium)

Fifty year peace with Byzantium

E G Y P T

Monks said to have smuggled in
silkworms and mulberry leaves
from Central Asia c.552

0   200
Miles

Index of Place Names[1]

Modern names are given in brackets

[1] I have sometimes sacrificed consistency of spelling to convenience and tradition.